# Introdu

**N**o matter where you turned in 1905, you coul... gar centenary. Manufacturers of ceramics and postcards, publishers and print makers have all left their mark. Centenary souvenirs are as much sought after now as items of Trafalgar itself - and they have the advantage of being cheaper to collectors. Although the last survivors of Nelson's navy were by then gone, there were sufficient numbers of people (not forgetting descendants) who knew these men. For the people of 1905, Trafalgar was recent history - almost in living memory. The demand for knowledge about Nelson, Trafalgar and Emma Hamilton resulted in countless reprints and new works and this included magazine articles. The sum total of this renewed focus led to a gradual reappraisal of Nelson's life and the people around him.

This anthology is derived from *T.P.'s Weekly,* a popular weekly magazine of general interest; the magazine ran from 1902 to the late 1920s. The founder was Irishman Thomas Power O'Connor (1848 - 1929), a journalist and MP, and the first president of the Board of Film Censors in 1917. The anthology is actually a collection of notes and queries which ran for 18 weeks in 1905. It is unashamedly reprinted in full without abridgement or comment. Doubtless readers will find here material that they have already read - quotations from Southey and Mahan are common for example. Some of the anecdotes are perhaps spurious or fanciful, but it is certain that there will be something here that is new for even the most expert of Nelson aficionados.

This is what people were reading in the centenary year of Trafalgar. Welcome to the world of 1905.

*David Shannon*
*Trafalgar Day 1999*

# 1805. NELSONIANA. 1905.

### Nelson's Sense of Fame—His Pre-Death Coffin—The Wine-Smuggler —A Neat Anagram.

In October the Centenary of the Battle of Trafalgar and the death of Nelson will be celebrated throughout the country with no ordinary feelings. Trafalgar remains the greatest naval event in European history, and it stands for our national existence, as its victorious admiral is our national hero.

I propose to give my readers a series of facts and anecdotes relating to Lord Nelson, to Trafalgar, and to the men and battles of that great period. While few of the stories I present can be new, many of them, I believe, will be unfamiliar. I do not propose to arrange them in chronological order; I shall rather present them as a miscellany at once varied, stirring, and curious, which will be continued from week to week.

## Charles Lamb on Nelson.

It is curious that we are able to associate two such different men as Charles Lamb and Lord Nelson. But on hearing the news of Nelson's glorious death Lamb wrote to Hazlitt: "Wasn't you sorry for Lord Nelson? I have followed him in fancy ever since I saw him walking in Pall Mall (I was prejudiced against him before), looking just like a hero should look; and I have been very much cut about it indeed. He was the only pretence of a Great Man we had. Nobody is left of any Name at all."

## An Ironical Uncle.

When Horatio was only twelve years of age, being at home during the Christmas Holidays, he read in the county newspaper that his uncle was appointed to the Raisonnable, of sixty-four guns. "Do, William," said he to a brother who was a year and a half older than himself, "write to my father, and tell him that I should like to go to sea with Uncle Maurice." Accordingly

Captain Suckling was written to. "What," said he in his answer, "has poor Horatio done, who is so weak, that he, above all the rest, should be sent to rough it out at sea? But let him come, and the first time we go into action a cannon-ball may knock off his head, and provide for him at once."

## Nelson's Sense of Fame.

Nelson had at all times a full and proper sense of his own value and of the fame he was earning. He frankly desired fame and the name of a hero. This is illustrated in the story which Benjamin West, President of the Royal Academy, told to George Ticknor in his studio in Newman Street. West's great picture of the death of Nelson was on the walls, and the artist told this story concerning it. Just before he went to sea for the last time, West sat next to him at a large entertainment given to him here, and in the course of the dinner Nelson expressed to Sir William Hamilton his regret, that in his youth he had not acquired some taste for art, and some power of discrimination. "But," said he, turning to West, "there is one picture whose power I do feel. I never pass a paint-shop where your ' Death of Wolfe ' is in the window, without being stopped by it." West, of course, made his acknowledgments, and Nelson went on to ask why he had painted no more like it. "Because, my lord, there are no more subjects." "D——n it," said the sailor, "I didn't think of that," and asked him to take a glass of champagne. "But, my lord, I fear your intrepidity will yet furnish me with such another scene; and, if it should, I shall certainly avail myself of it." "Will you?" said Nelson, pouring out bumpers, and touching his glass violently against West's—"will you, Mr. West? Then I hope that I shall die in the next battle." He sailed a few days after, and the result was on the canvas before us.

## Nelson's Pre-Death Coffin.

No present sent to Nelson, after the battle of the Nile, was so extraordinary as that which he received from his gallant friend Captain Hallowell, of the Swiftsure; and the idea could have occurred only to a very original mind. After L'Orient blew up, part of her mainmast was taken on board of the Swiftsure; and in May, 1799, Captain Hallowell, fearing the effect of all the praise and flattery lavished on his chief, determined to remind him that he was mortal. He therefore ordered a coffin to be made out of part of L'Orient's mast; and was so careful that nothing whatever should be used in its construction that was not taken from it, that the staples were formed of the spikes drawn from the cheeks of the mast, which were driven into the edge of the coffin; and when the lid was put on, toggles were put into the staples to keep it down, so as to prevent the necessity of using nails or screws for that purpose. The nails in the coffin were likewise made from the spikes taken from the mast. A paper was pasted on the bottom, containing the following certificate: "I do hereby certify that every part of this coffin is made of the wood and iron of L'Orient, most of which was picked up by His Majesty's ship under my command, in the Bay of Aboukir.—Swiftsure, May 23, 1799.—Ben Hallowell." This singular present was accompanied by the following letter, which is taken from the original in the "Nelson Papers"; a fact it is necessary to state, because both Charnock and Harrison, not contented with destroying its simplicity, altered the address to "Sir," and changed the date to "August, 1798," to make it appear that the coffin was sent immediately after the battle of the Nile. Though printed correctly by Clarke and M'Arthur, Southey followed the copy given by Charnock and Harrison. It is greatly to be regretted that Nelson's reply has not been found:

The Right Hon. Lord Nelson, K.B.
My Lord,—Herewith I send you a coffin made of part of L'Orient's mainmast; that when you are tired of this life you may be buried in one of your own trophies; but may that period be far distant, is the sincere wish of your obedient and much obliged servant,
BEN HALLOWELL.
Swiftsure, May 23, 1799.

The astonishment that prevailed among the crew of the Vanguard, Lord Nelson's flag-ship, when they were convinced it was a coffin which had been brought on board, was for long remembered by their officers. "We shall have hot work of it, indeed!" said one of the seamen; "you see the Admiral intends to fight till he is killed, and there he is to be buried." Lord Nelson highly appreciated the present, and for some time had it placed upright, with the lid on, against the bulk-head of his cabin behind the chair on which he sat at dinner. At length, by the entreaties of an old servant, he was prevailed on to allow it to be carried below. When his lordship left the Vanguard, the coffin was removed into the Foudroyant, where it remained for many days on the gratings of the quarter-deck. While his officers were one day looking at it, he came out of the cabin: "You may look at it, gentlemen," said he, "as long as you please; but, depend on it, none of you shall have it." It is satisfactory to state that Nelson was actually buried in this coffin.—"Nelson's Despatches, Letters, &c., with Notes by Sir N. H. Nicolas."

---

## Lord Nelson's Nightcap.

Doctor Burney, who wrote the celebrated anagram on Lord Nelson after his victory of the Nile, "Honor est a Nilo" (Horatio Nelson), was, shortly after, on a visit to Nelson at Merton. From his usual absence of mind, he forgot to put a nightcap into his portmanteau, and consequently borrowed one from his host. Previous to his retiring to rest, he sat down to study, as was his common practice, and was shortly after alarmed by finding the cap in flames; he immediately collected the burnt remains, and returned them to Nelson with the following lines:

Take your nightcap again, my good lord, I
   desire;
I would not detain it a minute;
What belongs to a Nelson, where'er there's
   a fire,
Is sure to be instantly in it.

---

## Saved from an Error

At twenty-two Nelson found himself in Quebec, and here he formed an unwise attachment, from which he was only saved by a brother officer more resolute even than himself. This was Alexander Davison. Nelson's ship, the

Albemarle, was about to leave the station; her captain had taken leave of his friends, and was gone down the river to the place of anchorage; when, the next morning, as Davison was walking along the beach, to his surprise he saw Nelson coming back in his boat. Upon inquiring the cause of this reappearance, Nelson took his arm to walk towards the town, and told him he found it utterly impossible to leave Quebec without again seeing the woman whose society had contributed so much to his happiness there and offering her his hand. "If you do," said his friend, "your utter ruin must inevitably follow." "Then let it follow," cried Nelson, "for I am resolved to do it." "And I," replied Davison, "am resolved you shall not." Nelson, however, upon this occasion, was less resolute than his friend, and suffered himself to be led back to the boat.

## The Last Signal.

Here are the words as conveyed by signal at Trafalgar, and as noted down by several ships in the fleet:

| England | expects | that | every | man | will | do | his | d | u | t | y |
|---|---|---|---|---|---|---|---|---|---|---|---|
| 253 | 269 | 863 | 261 | 471 | 958 | 220 | 370 | 4 | 21 | 19 | 24 |

I am aware that the precise words of Nelson's signal are in dispute, and I shall produce the particulars of the discussion in a future number.

## Nelson and Children.

At a splendid party given by Lord Hamilton to the Prince of Wales, &c., I saw Lady Hamilton go through all those "attitudes" which have been engraved; and her performance was very beautiful indeed. Her husband, Sir William, was present.

Lord Nelson was a remarkably kind-hearted man. I have seen him spin a teetotum with his one hand, a whole evening, for the amusement of some children. I heard him once during dinner utter many bitter complaints (which Lady Hamilton vainly attempted to check) of the way he had been treated at court that forenoon; the Queen had not condescended to take the slightest notice of him. In truth, Nelson was hated at court; they were jealous of his fame.

There was something very charming in Lady Hamilton's openness of manner. She showed me the neckcloth which Nelson had on when he died. Of course, I could not help looking at it with extreme interest; and she threw her arms round my neck and kissed me. She was latterly in great want; and Lord Stowell never rested till he procured for her a small pension from Government.—Rogers's "Table Talk."

## Nelson and the Wine Smuggler.

A correspondent of the "European Magazine," October, 1807, told the following: While cruising off Cadiz, Lord Nelson's boats took a Spanish polacre laden with wine, &c., and from which one of his seamen contrived to smuggle on board a small cask. While, however, he was conveying it to his berth, his lordship, observing him, called out, "What, Jack, not ask your old commander to have a drop; you know I'd not serve you so." Jack, who expected nothing less than a round dozen, now advanced, with an awkward bow, presented it to his lordship, and requested him to drink. The hero, with his usual condescension, accepted it, and calling for glasses, with his officers and the seaman, drank, "Success to the British fleet," amid the repeated shouts of the remainder of his gallant followers. He then dismissed Jack with his wine, and a reprimand, "Never to be so ill-natured again."

4

# 1805. NELSONIANA. 1905.

### Nelson's Hat—Wellington meets Him—The Little Viscountess— A Liverpool Eulogy.

## Resolves to be a Hero.

As a young man Nelson suffered much from ill-health. He had to be brought home from India as the only chance of saving his life, and the sight of brother-officers beginning their careers in health and vigour threw him into something like despair. "I felt impressed," said he, "with a feeling that I should never rise in my profession. My mind was staggered with a view of the difficulties I had to surmount, and the little interest I possessed. I could discover no means of reaching the object of my ambition. After a long and gloomy reverie, in which I almost wished myself overboard, a sudden glow of patriotism was kindled within me, and presented my king and country as my patron. 'Well, then,' I exclaimed, 'I will be a hero, and, confiding in Providence, I will brave every danger!'"

## Nelson on German Generals.

It is interesting at this time to recall Lord Nelson's opinion of the German generals, as expressed by him in 1795:

As for the German generals, war is their trade, and peace is ruin to them; therefore we cannot expect that they should have any wish to finish the war.

These words were remembered as sadly applicable in the year 1871; let us hope that they are not again to become appropriate.

## Nelson's Hat.

A writer in "Notes and Queries" of November 17, 1883, writes: While Maclise was painting, in the Royal Gallery at Westminster, the "Interview of Wellington and Blucher" and the "Death of Nelson," I often stayed to gossip with the artist while he worked upon the walls. On one occasion he lamented that, having taken no end of pains to verify the costumes of his soldiers and sailors, he had never been able to get hold of a hat of Nelson's such as he wished to represent on or near the dying admiral in the latter design. Bearing in mind the costume of the effigy in question, which I had often studied, remembering that it included a cocked hat, and having no doubt that the whole suit had belonged to Nelson at the period of his death, I told Maclise that he had only to cross the street to secure what he coveted. "Why, in Heaven's name, didn't you tell me so before?" cried he, jumping up. "How could I know you wanted it?" was the return query. Instantly we set off. Maclise saw Dean Stanley, who caused the glass case of the effigy to be opened, and there, sure enough, we found not only the very thing the artist craved for, but the strongest presumptive evidence that the hat at least, if not, as was most probable, the entire suit which clothes the figure, had belonged to, and even been worn by, the admiral. Grease and sweat marks stain that part of the lining of the hat which had touched the wearer's head, except where the edge of the eye-patch attached to the inner rim of the lining had protected that lining. There the patch itself is soiled. The maker's name is inside the hat as usual, together with the stamp acknowledging the payment of the tax on the garment. I forget the name of the maker, but remember that his address was somewhere in St. James's Street. Maclise borrowed the hat and painted from it.

## Wellington describes Nelson.

The following intensely interesting conversation took place at Walmer Castle on October 1, 1834. We were talking (says John Wilson Croker) of Lord Nelson, and some instances were mentioned of the egotism and vanity that derogated from his character.

"Why," said the Duke, "I am not surprised at such instances, for Lord Nelson was, in different circumstances, two quite different men, as I myself can vouch, though I only saw him once in my life, and for, perhaps, an hour. It was soon after I returned from India. I went to the Colonial Office in Downing Street, and there I was shown into the little waiting-room on the right hand, where I found, also waiting to see the Secretary of State, a gentleman, whom, from his likeness to his pictures and the loss of an arm, I immediately recognised as Lord Nelson.

"He could not know who I was, but he entered at once into conversation with me, if I can call it conversation, for it was almost all on his side, and all about himself, and in really a style so vain and so silly as to surprise and almost disgust me. I suppose something that I happened to say may have made him guess that I was somebody, and he went out of the room for a moment, I have no doubt to ask the office-keeper who I was, for when he came back he was altogether a different man, both in manner and matter. All that I had thought a charlatan style had vanished, and he talked of the state of this country and of the aspect and probabilities of affairs on the Continent with a good sense, and a knowledge of subjects both at home and abroad, that surprised me equally and more agreeably than the first part of our interview had done; in fact, he talked like an officer and a statesman.

"The Secretary of State kept us long waiting, and certainly for the last half or three-quarters of an hour I don't know that I ever had a conversation that interested me more. Now, if the Secretary of State had been punctual, and admitted Lord Nelson in the first quarter of an hour, I should have had the same impression of a light and trivial character that other people have had, but luckily I saw enough to be satisfied that he was really a very superior man; but certainly a more sudden and complete metamorphosis I never saw."

## Links with Nelson.

It would be interesting to know what links can be established between living people and Lord Nelson. Sir George Trevelyan is able to recall a nurse who remembered seeing, when a factory girl at Coventry, Nelson and Lady Hamilton in that town. Perhaps a few of my readers can establish such links.

## An Incident after Copenhagen.

During the repast given by the Crown Prince of Denmark to Lord Nelson, after the battle of Copenhagen, and the preliminaries of peace were adjusted, Nelson spoke in raptures of the bravery of the Danes, and particularly requested the Prince to introduce him to a very young officer, whom he described as having performed wonders during the battle, by attacking his own ship immediately under her lower guns.

It proved to be a gallant young fellow named Welmos, a stripling of seventeen. The British hero embraced him with the enthusiasm of a brother, and delicately intimated to the Prince that he ought to make him an admiral; to which the Prince very happily replied, "If, my lord, I were to make all my brave officers admirals, I should have no captains or lieutenants in my service." This heroic youth had volunteered the command of a "praam," a sort of raft, carrying six small cannon, and manned with twenty-four men. He and his small crew pushed off from the shore, and, in the fury of the battle, placed themselves under the stern of Lord Nelson's ship, which they attacked in such a manner that, though they were below the reach of the stern chasers, the British marines made terrible slaughter amongst them; twenty of these gallant men fell by their bullets, but their young commander continued knee-deep in dead at his post until the truce was announced.

---

## The Little Viscountess.

The widow of our great Admiral (says Mrs. Hilda Gamlin, in her very interesting work, "Nelson's Friendships") mostly resided at fashionable watering places or inland summer haunts frequented by the best society, such as Brighton or Clifton, and for some years in the first quarter of this century she resided at 8, The Beacon, Exmouth, Devon. The house she occupied was in the best situation, whence a lovely view of the sea and the Devonshire coast could be obtained; it was the largest in a terrace, a long, low house, with really good rooms, and still is occupied by persons in good condition of life.

It is strange that portraits of Lady Nelson are so scarce; indeed, it has often been said that there was no portrait of her in existence, yet she was acquainted with Sir William Beechey and with Abbott, and a few lines in the Morrison Collection of MSS. written by her show that she was interested in fine art: "Lady Nelson will be obliged to Mr. Mead to allow her the pleasure of showing his portraits, &c., to some of her friends to-morrow at 1 o'clock." She was petite in figure, and Mrs. Matcham used to refer to her as "the little Viscountess."

## A Touching Eulogy from Liverpool.

The following touching tribute to Nelson was written by a Liverpool man shortly after the hero's death. It refers to Nelson's expressed intention to visit Liverpool:

"As a sailor, and the chief of sailors, he was a special favourite in this sea-port town; his name was among our 'household words'; his life, a thousand romances in one reality, was the popular theme at every table and round every fire. Wellington was in the bud then, and all the talk was of Nelson—nothing but Nelson. When, therefore, the account of his death was received there was not a man in Liverpool but wished with all his heart and soul the victory unwon, and the departed hero yet alive and spared to us. It seemed, so intense was the feeling of regret, as if the destroying Angel had again passed through the land as of old through Egypt, and taken one from every house. Grief was in every family, lamentation in every circle, sorrow in every countenance. These feelings were the more intense in Liverpool, inasmuch as the intelligence of the hero's death followed close upon a letter from himself, in which he announced his intion, as he had never yet seen the 'good old town,' of paying it a visit as soon as he had 'settled his small account' with the French and Spanish Fleets, which he was then blockading in Cadiz. How uncertain are the events of this life! We wept the hero dead whom we hoped to welcome in all the pride and brilliancy of his glory! The envelope that contained this letter hung for many a year in a splendid frame in the dining-room of a leading Liverpool gentleman."

# 1805.  NELSONIANA.  1905.

### The Battle of St. Vincent—An Anagram—The Lobiolly Boy.

### The Battle of St. Vincent (I).

This great battle, fought in February, 1797, afforded Nelson one of the many opportunities which came to him of exercising a bold intelligence in advance of that possessed by his superior, who in this case was, of course, the gallant Jervis. This admiral did not order the complete chase which was feasible, and which would have resulted in the capture of the entire Spanish fleet. Nelson, in command of the Captain, threw himself in the way of its retreat, and was at one time engaged with nine ships of the enemy. In the result four Spanish ships were taken. Both Jervis and Nelson show well in the pages of Clark Russell's "Horatio Nelson." We read:

The British Admiral Jervis made the signal to prepare for battle. As he walked the quarter-deck the hostile numbers were reported to him, as they appeared, by signal.

"There are eight sail-of-the-line, Sir John."

"Very well, sir."

"There are twenty sail-of-the-line, Sir John."

"Very well, sir."

"There are twenty-five sail-of-the-line."

"Very well, sir."

"There are twenty-seven sail-of-the line, Sir John," and this was accompanied by some remark on the great disparity of the forces.

"Enough, sir!—no more of that! The die is cast, and if there were fifty sail I would go through them."

## The Battle of St. Vincent (2).

Captain Hallowell, who was at Jervis's side when he thus spoke, was so delighted by this determined answer that, gently clapping the old Admiral on his back, he cried out, "That's right, Sir John, that's right! By G—, we shall give them a d——d good licking!" At close upon half-past eleven o'clock Jervis hoisted his large flag and ensign, and, announcing his intention to pass through the enemy's line, ran aloft the signal to engage. The action was soon general. The Spaniards were unable to unite their divided ships, and those to leeward presently put about and went stretching away in search of safety. Jervis, having effected his first purpose, signalled for the British fleet to tack in succession. It was then seen that the Spanish Admiral's plan was to join his leeward ships by wearing round under the sterns of the rearward of the British line. Nelson's genius penetrated the Don's intention, and, putting the Captain's helm hard-a-weather, he steered a course for the enemy.

The sixth ship from the Spaniards' rear was that towering four-decker the Santissima Trinidad, of one hundred and thirty-six guns. Nelson got alongside of her, but ahead and astern of him were the Don's seconds of three decks each. Troubridge, in the Culloden, headed with all possible speed to his assistance, and was presently followed by Frederick, in the Blenheim. Nelson's instant, intrepid resolution staggered the Spanish admiral. The fire of the British was overwhelming, and such was its effect upon the enemy's ships that the little crowd of onlookers on board the Lively, even in an early moment of the conflict, foresaw a glorious termination to the battle.

---

## The Battle of St. Vincent (3).

Nelson is the one conspicuous figure in that scene of roaring ordnance, of banks of powder smoke smitten by the red flashes of murderously-plied batteries, of falling spars, of the shrieks of the dying and the wounded, and the stormy huzzas of the English sailors, wrestling half-naked at their guns. At one moment the Captain was engaged with no less than nine line-of-battle ships. A little later on she was hammering at the San Josef and the San Nicolas. The latter luffed, the San Josef fell aboard her, the Captain being abreast of them and close alongside. Her fore-topmast was gone, her wheel was shot away, her running-rigging was in pieces; and Nelson, perceiving that she was no longer manageable, manœuvred so as to foul the San Nicolas. This he contrived. His spritsail yard hooked the San Nicolas's rigging. There were a number of the 69th regiment on board, and they were amongst the first who sprang into the Don—no easy task to landsmen encumbered with weapons, with the long Atlantic swell besides to create swift abysses between the roaring and flaming fabrics as they rolled.

Colonel Bethuse, after the action, had a chat with Nelson, and asked, "How came you to get into that singular and perilous situation?" "I'll tell you how it happened," he answered. "The Admiral's intention, I saw, was to cut off the detached squadron of light sail, and afterwards attack the main body, weakened by the separation. Observing, however, as our squadron advanced and became engaged with the enemy's ships, that the main body of the enemy were pushing to join their friends to leeward by passing in the rear of our squadron, I thought unless by some prompt and extraordinary measure the main body could be diverted from this course until Sir John (at that time in action on the Victory) could see their plan, his well-arranged designs on the enemy would be frustrated." His resolution was immediately formed, with what success we have seen.

---

## Lady Hamilton.

We know few characters (says an excellent writer in "Blackwood" of April, 1860—and his words have lost little weight since then) of which it is so difficult to form a just and impartial estimate as that of Lady Hamilton. Happily it is not our duty to mete out reward or punishment. Few, if any, have ever been exposed to such dangers and such temptations. The most precious gifts of Providence, bodily and mental, which were lavished upon her in profusion, were but so many additional snares in her path. "With all her faults," says one who was by no means disposed to extenuate these faults, "her goodness of heart is undeniable. She was the frequent intercessor with Nelson for offending sailors; and in every vicissitude of her fortune she manifested the warmest affection for her mother, and showed the greatest kindness to a host of discreditable relations." Her husband, with his dying breath, bore witness that, during "the ten years of their happy union, she had never, in thought, word, or deed, offended him."

The nature of her intimacy with Nelson will probably remain for ever an enigma. The more closely the evidence is examined, the more perplexing does the inquiry become. Confident assertion in this, as in most other cases, is confined almost exclusively to those who know least of the subject. There cannot be a stronger proof of this difficulty than that which is derived from the fact that the two latest biographers of Nelson, both of whom have devoted infinite labour to the inquiry, have arrived at diametrically opposite conclusions. Dr. Pettigrew is convinced that Horatia was the daughter of Lady Hamilton, and Sir Harris Nicolas is equally convinced that she was not. Those who were most likely to be well-informed upon the subject, Lord St. Vincent, Hardy, Dr. Scott, his confidential friend and adviser Mr. Haslewood, and, we may add, the several members of his own family, seem to have considered Nelson's attachment to Lady Hamilton purely platonic. The evidence in support of this view of the case is collected in the seventh volume of the "Nelson Despatches," pp. 369 to 396.-"Blackwood's Magazine," April, 1860.

---

## "The Neatest Anagram Extant."

The following anagram is, in the opinion of a writer of 1807, the neatest and most pointed one extant. The Christian and surname of the hero of the Nile and Trafalgar make exactly the following Latin words:

*Honor est a Nilo.*
Honour is from the Nile.

Thirteen letters, exactly the same as in the name of Horatio Nelson, which forms a happy coincidence and allusion; for had he been christened Horace, or Horatius, the anagram could not be made. As it is, it is, perhaps, the happiest and most complete that ever was produced; and it is attributed to Dr. Burney, of Greenwich. Had this anagram been previously discovered, it might well have been a motto for Nelson's arms, equally, if not more suitable than the one he adopted at the suggestion of Pitt: *Palmam qui meruit ferat* (Let him bear the palm who has deserved it).

---

## Lord Nelson and Jack Rider the Loblolly Boy.

Jack was what they call loblolly boy on board the Victory. It was his duty to do anything and everything that was required—from sweeping and washing the deck, and saying "Amen" to the chaplain, down to cleaning the guns, and helping the doctor to make pills and plasters, and mix medicines. Four days before the battle that was so glorious to England, but so fatal to its greatest hero, Jack was ordered by the doctor to fetch a bottle that was standing in a particular place. Jack ran off, post haste, to the spot, where he found what appeared to be an empty bottle. Curiosity was uppermost; "What," thought Jack, "can there be about this empty bottle?" He examined it carefully, but couldn't comprehend the mystery, so he thought that he would call in the aid of a candle, to throw light on the subject. The bottle contained ether, and the result of the examination was that the vapour ignited, and the flames extended to some of the sails, and also to a part of the ship. There was a general confusion—running with buckets and what not—and, to make matters worse, the fire was rapidly extending to the powder magazine. During the hubbub, Lord Nelson was in the chief cabin writing dispatches. His lordship heard the noise—he couldn't do otherwise—and so, in a loud voice, he called out, "What's all that d——d noise about?" The boatswain answered, "My Lord, the loblolly boy's set fire to an empty bottle, and it's set fire to the ship." "Oh!" said Nelson, "that's all, is it? I thought the enemy had boarded us and taken us all prisoners—you and loblolly must put it out, and take care we're not blown up! but pray make as little noise about it as you can, or I can't go on with my despatches," and with these words Nelson went to his desk, and continued his writing with the greatest coolness.—Dixon's "Stories of the Craven Dales."

## Why He Stole the Pears.

Of Nelson's boyhood some familiar stories are told. Everyone knows how he told his grandmother in all simplicity that he had never seen fear: "What is it?" Another story, told by Southey, is less often quoted. There were some fine pears growing in the schoolmaster's garden, which the boys regarded as lawful booty, and in the highest degree tempting; but the boldest among them were afraid to venture for the prize. Horatio volunteered upon this service; he was lowered down at night from the bedroom window by some sheets, plundered the tree, was drawn up with the pears, and then distributed them among his schoolfellows without reserving any for himself. "He only took them," he said, "because every other boy was afraid."

## "Horace."

When Nelson was between nine and eleven years of age he twice accompanied his father to church to act as witness to marriages. The first occasion on which he thus signed his name he did so in a carefully-rounded schoolboy hand; but on the second time he put a little more dash into it, and wrongly subscribed his Christian name, for he wrote, "Horace Nelson," thus showing that he was more frequently called Horace than Horatio by his relatives. The precise rector, however, corrected the error, for in the register the "ce" is erased and "tio" written above in big characters.

## July 28, 1905.

# 1805. NELSONIANA. 1905.

## The Nelson Column (1).

Who was "J. B.," to whom belongs the honour of having suggested, in a letter to the "Times" of September 9, 1837, the desirability of adorning Trafalgar Square with a worthy monument to Lord Nelson? History, so far as I know, is dumb, though I suppose no letter to the "Times" has been more successful. For in the same newspaper of April 27, 1838, appeared the following notice:

NELSON MONUMENT.—The committee for erecting a monument to the memory of Lord Nelson hereby give notice that they are desirous of receiving from architects, artists, and other persons, designs for such a monument, to be erected in Trafalgar Square.

The committee cannot, in the present state of the subscriptions, fix definitely the sum to be expended, but they recommend that the estimated cost of the several designs should be confined within the sum of £20,000 to £30,000. This condition, and that of the intended site, are the only restrictions to which artists are limited.

But the project moved slowly, and another year passed before the designs were adjudicated.

## The Nelson Column (2).

In April, 1839, the "Gentleman's Magazine" was able to report the result of the competition. This it did as follows:

The designs of the competitors for the Nelson Memorial, 124 in number, have been publicly exhibited at Mr. Rainy's gallery in Regent Street, the three prizes having been previously assigned by the Committee. It is generally agreed that the designs, on the whole, betray a lamentable deficiency of invention, and that by far the larger majority are conceived without adequate reference to the intended site (the vast area of Trafalgar Square) or to the surrounding buildings.

The first premium was adjudged by the Committee to the proposition of W. Railton, architect, for a fluted Corinthian column, 174 feet high, on a pedestal ornamented with reliefs, and surmounted by a statue 17 feet high. This design can, of course, make no pretension to originality; and besides is open to various other objections.

The second prize is that of a sculptor, Mr. E. H. Baily, R.A. It has been generally admired for its classical grace, consisting of a group of three colossal figures, and a triumphal procession of Neptune and other marine deities encircling the pedestal. It would be an exceedingly beautiful work within a temple ; but its size would be very insignificant in the great area of Trafalgar Square, at the same time that its execution in even the proposed dimensions would be exceedingly expensive (in marble £22,000 in bronze £30,000).

The third prize is assigned to a joint design of Mr. Charles Fowler, architect, and Mr. R. W. Sievier, sculptor. This erection is proposed to be 120 feet ; a statue of Nelson is placed on a pedestal adorned with rostra and a variety of other appropriate ornaments, and seated against its four fronts are colossal statues of Britannia, Caledonia, Hibernia, and Neptune. Estimate £25,000.

The Committee have subsequently resolved to return all the designs, leaving it to the several candidates and to others to alter and amend the old or furnish new ones, and submit them to a fresh selection.

---

## The Nelson Column (3).

On April 10, 1840, the offer of Messrs. Guisell and Peto to erect the Column within two years, for a sum of £17,860, was accepted. The foundation stone, strange to say, was laid without ceremony. This was on September 30, 1840. Despite the terms of the contract it was three years before the raising of Baily's statue to the summit was begun. The figure, which stood 17 feet high, and weighed eighteen tons, was made of stone from the Duke of Buccleugh's Granton quarry. It was, of course, in segments, but these were put together on the ground so that the public might inspect the complete work. In the two days during which it was on view it was visited by 100,000 persons. The following is a contemporary account of the elevation of the statue to its present position :

*Nov.* 4.—The statue of Lord Nelson, by Baily, reached its destination on the top of the column, erected under the management and after the design of Mr. Railton. The lower part was got up on Friday morning, after six hours' labour, and the upper portion followed on Saturday morning, and the arm was also in the course of the day united to the body.

A flag-staff was erected which reached above the head of the figure, and from it was displayed the Union Jack, which is the identical flag under which the hero fell at the battle of Trafalgar.

This figure breathes the very soul and spirit of Nelson ; there we behold the intrepid firmness of his mind—the determination to achieve his purpose, unawed by any terrors which the foes of his country could evoke. The simplicity of the attitude is very striking : here is no extended hand with truncheon or with telescope ; it is Nelson himself on his quarterdeck, cool and collected. Like the Angel introduced in Addison's Campaign, as an emblem of Marlborough's imperturbed spirit—calm and serene, he drives the furious blast of battle ; rides in the whirlwind and directs the storm ; and of Nelson it might indeed be truly added, from the same source,

In joys of conquest he resigned his breath,
And, filled with England's glory, smiled in death.

Even when his life-blood was ebbing from his wound, reducing to a few short moments the current of his existence, Nelson's spirit was still active for his country's cause, still busied in the direction of his fleet. Assured of victory and of the capture and destruction of the foe, his dying words were—" *Then let us anchor !* "

---

## Links with Nelson.

In response to my remark that it would be interesting to know of links between living people and Nelson, Miss Sarah Barker, of Dawley, Shropshire, sends me this interesting communication :

"During the eighties I was on terms of warm friendship with a remarkable and accomplished lady who resided in the city of Worcester, Miss Theodosia Yeomans Egan, whose delight it was to recall the spectacle she witnessed at Greenwich as a child, viz., the bringing of the body of Nelson to the shore. Lifted to a window-sill by the hands of a kindly stranger, who saw the peril of the young child in the surging crowd (she had escaped from the garden of her father, Dr. Egan, unnoticed by her attendants), she beheld one of the most moving scenes in history, to recall it with vividness in extreme old age, to the young girl who was never weary of hearing the story. Miss Egan, who stood in the relationship of aunt to Mr. Fletcher Moulton, K.C., died at Winchester in

1892, within a few months of completing her hundredth year."

An "Old Naval Officer" writes that many years ago, about the years 1859-60, he was serving on the Mediterranean, and at that time there lived an old Mons. Collet, who was said to have been a spy for Nelson. He certainly had seen him, and had many curious anecdotes about Nelson et Bronté, as he always called him. At the time this old Naval Officer joined the Service during the Russian War, there were several Trafalgar officers still serving afloat.

Mr. Ramsay Parsons writes from Kensington:

"I have no recollection of the fact, but when a very young child I played with my grandfather, or rather he with me. He was one of Lord Nelson's midshipmen on board the fighting Foudroyant, and the one told off to wait on the King of Naples when on board that vessel. He was the author of 'Nelsonian Reminiscences.'"

## The Walrus.

The story of Nelson and the walrus (some versions make the animal a bear) is well known, but is worth re-telling. The incident occurred during the voyage in search of the North Pole, undertaken at the instance of the Royal Society, by the "Racehorse" and the "Carcass." During the ice operations Nelson, young as he was, received the command of one of the boats which were sent to explore a passage in the open water. Some of the officers (says Southey) had fired at and wounded a walrus. As no other animal has so human-like an expression in its countenance, so also is there none that seems to possess more of the passions of humanity. The wounded animal dived immediately, and brought up a number of its companions, and they all joined in an attack upon the boat. They wrested an oar from one of the men, and it was with the utmost difficulty that the crew could prevent them from staving or upsetting her till the "Carcass's" boat came up; and the walruses, finding their enemies thus reinforced, dispersed. Young Nelson exposed himself in a more daring manner. One night, during the mid-watch, he stole from the ship with one of his comrades, taking advantage of a rising fog, and set off over the ice in pursuit of a bear. It was not long before they were missed. The fog thickened, and Captain Lutwidge and his officers became exceedingly alarmed for their safety. Between three and four in the morning the weather cleared, and the two adventurers were seen, at a considerable distance from the ship, attacking a huge bear. The signal for them to return was immediately made; Nelson's comrade called upon him to obey it, but in vain; his musket had flashed in the pan; their ammunition was expended; and a chasm in the ice, which divided him from the bear, probably preserved his life. "Never mind," he cried; "do but let me get a blow at this devil with the butt-end of my musket, and we shall have him." Captain Lutwidge, however, seeing his danger, fired a gun, which had the desired effect of frightening the beast; and the boy then returned, somewhat afraid of the consequences of his trespass. The Captain reprimanded him sternly for conduct so unworthy of the office which he filled, and desired to know what motive he could have for hunting a bear. "Sir," said he, pouting his lip, as he was wont to do when agitated, "I wished to kill the bear that I might carry the skin to my father."

## George Borrow in Trafalgar Bay.

It is in the fifty-first chapter of that wonderful book, "The Bible in Spain," that George Borrow gives his impressions of Trafalgar Bay:

"In about two hours we passed the Castle of Santa Petra, and at noon were in sight of Trafalgar. The wind now freshened, and was dead ahead, on which account we hugged closely to the coast, in order to avoid as much as possible the strong heavy sea which was pouring down from the Straits. We passed within a very short distance of the Cape, a bold bluff foreland, but not of any considerable height.

"It is impossible for an Englishman to pass by this place—the scene of the most celebrated naval action on record—without emotion. Here it was that the united navies of France and Spain were annihilated by a far inferior force; but that force was British, and was directed by one of the most remarkable men of the age, and perhaps the greatest hero of any time. Huge fragments of wreck still frequently emerge from the watery gulf whose billows chafe the rocky sides of Trafalgar: they are relics of the enormous ships which were burnt and sunk on that terrible day, when the heroic champion of Britain concluded his work and died. I never heard but one individual venture to say a word in disparagement of Nelson's glory: it was a pert American, who observed that the British Admiral was much overrated. 'Can that individual be overrated,' replied a stranger, 'whose every thought was bent on his country's honour, who scarcely ever fought without leaving a piece of his body in the fray, and who, not to speak of minor triumphs, was victorious in two such actions as Aboukir and Trafalgar?'"

## Nelson.

The great admiral's watchword before the battle of the Nile was "A peerage or Westminster Abbey." Wise men now commonly quote this: "Victory or Westminster Abbey"; as if Nelson ever doubted of victory; or as if, supposing he had not got the victory, he would have been likely to have been buried in Westminster Abbey.—H. G.

## August 4, 1905.

# 1805. NELSONIANA. 1905.

### Nelson and Wellington Descended from Edward I.

Lady Elizabeth Plantagenet daughter of King Edward I., married Humphrey de Bohun, Earl of Hereford and Essex, Lord High Constable of England, and left two daughters, Eleanor and Margaret—from the former, Nelson was 15th in a direct descent; and from the latter, Wellington, 14th. Thus:—

Lady Eleanor de Bohun (elder daughter and co-heir of Humphrey de Bohun, Earl of Hereford) became the wife of James Butler 1st Earl of Ormonde,

And had a son, James Butler, 2nd Earl of Ormonde, great-grandfather of Thomas, 7th Earl of Ormonde,

Whose second daughter and co-heir was Lady Margaret Butler, the wife of Sir William Boleyn, Kt.,

And the mother of Thomas Boleyn, Viscount Rochford, K.G.

This Thomas, Viscount (son of Lady Margaret Butler, and great-great-great-great-grandson of Lady Eleanor de Bohun), married Lady Elizabeth Howard,

And was father of Mary Boleyn (sister of Queen Anne Boleyn),

Who wedded Sir William Cary,

And had a son Henry Cary, Lord Hunsdon, K.G.,

Whose granddaughter, Blanche Cary, became the wife of Sir Thomas Wodehouse,

And the mother of Anne Wodehouse, who married Robert Suckling,

And was grandmother of Catherine Suckling, the wife of the Rev. Edmund Suckling,

And the mother of HORATIO LORD NELSON.

Lady Margaret de Bohun (second daughter and co-heir of Humphrey de Bohun, Earl of Hereford) married Hugh Courtenay, second Earl of Devon,

And was mother of Lady Margaret Courtenay, who wedded John, Lord Cobham,

And had a daughter, Joan Cobham. This lady became the wife of Sir John de la Pole,

And the mother of Joan de la Pole, Lady Cobham, who married Sir Reginald Braybrooke.

The only surviving child of this alliance was Joan Braybrooke, Lady Cobham, who married Sir Thomas Brooke, Kt.,

And their younger son, Reginald Brooke, of Aspal, had a daughter, Elizabeth Brooke, the wife of Francis Peyton, and the grandmother of Sir Christopher Peyton, Auditor-General of Ireland,

Whose only daughter and heir, Anne Peyton, married—first, Sir Richard Cooke ; and, secondly, Sir Henry Colley,

By the latter husband she left a son, Dudley Colley, M.P., who was great-great-grandfather of Arthur, DUKE OF WELLINGTON.

### Spoiled for Fishermen.

The following anecdote is from Sir Walter Scott's "Quarterly Review" article on Sir Humphry Davy's "Salmonia":—

"The author of Salmonia," writes Sir Walter, "mentions Nelson's fondness for fly-fishing, and expresses a wish to see it noticed in the next edition of 'that most exquisite and touching life of our Hero by the Laureate, an immortal monument raised by genius to valour.' We believe neither Haliœus—one of the characters in 'Salmonia'—nor the Laureate will be displeased with the following little anecdote from a letter of a gentleman, now at the head of the medical profession, with which he favoured us shortly after perusing 'Salmonia': 'It was,' says our friend, 'the Naval Hospital at Yarmouth, on the morning when Nelson, after the battle of Copenhagen (having sent the wounded before him), arrived at the Roads, and landed on the jetty. The populace soon surounded him, and the military were drawn up in the market-place ready to receive him; but making his way through the crowd and the dust and the clamour, he went straight to the hospital. I went round the wards with him, and was much interested in observing his demeanour to the sailors; he stopped at every bed, and to every man he had something kind and cheery to say. At length he stopped opposite a bed on which a sailor was lying, who had lost his right arm close to the shoulder-joint, and the following short dialogue passed between them:

"'Nelson: "Well, Jack, what's the matter with you?"

"'Sailor: "Lost my arm, your honour."

"'Nelson paused, looked down at his own empty sleeve, then at the sailor, and said playfully: "Well, Jack, then you and I are spoiled for fishermen; cheer up, my brave fellow." And he passed briskly on to the next bed; but those few words had a magical effect on the poor fellow, for I saw his eyes sparkle with delight as Nelson turned away and pursued his course through the wards. As this was the only occasion on which I saw Nelson, I may, perhaps, overrate the value of the incident.'"

## Nelson and his Midshipmen.

One of Nelson's earliest commands was that of the Boreas, twenty-eight guns. The ship was full of young midshipmen, of whom (says Southey) there were not less than thirty on board; and happy were they whose lot it was to be placed with such a captain. If he perceived that a boy was afraid at first going aloft, he would say to him in a friendly manner, "Well, sir, I am going

a race to the mast-head, and beg that I may meet you there." The poor little fellow instantly began to climb, and got up how he could—Nelson never noticed in what manner; but, when they met in the top, spoke cheerfully to him, and would say how much any person was to be pitied who fancied that getting up was either dangerous or difficult. Every day he went into the schoolroom to see that they were pursuing their nautical studies, and at noon he was always the first on deck with his quadrant. Whenever he paid a visit of ceremony some of these youths accompanied him; and when he went to dine with the Governor at Barbadoes he took one of them in his hand and presented him, saying, "Your Excellency must excuse me for bringing one of my midshipmen. I make it a rule to introduce them to all the good company I can, as they have few to look up to, besides myself, during the time they are at sea."

## Trafalgar or Trafalgar.

The correct pronunciation is Trafal*g*ar. It must be used in Byron's references. Thus:

"The oak leviathans, whose huge ribs make
Their clay creator the vain title take
Of lord of thee, and arbiter of war;
These are thy toys, and, as the snowy flake,
They melt into thy yeast of waves, which mar
Alike the Armada's pride, or spoils of Trafalgár."

"Childe Harold."

"Nelson was once Britannia's god of war,
And still should be so, but the tide is turn'd;
There's no more to be said of Trafalgár,
'Tis with our hero quietly inurn'd,
Because the army's grown more popular,
At which the naval people are concern'd."

"Don Juan."

## A Memorable Sunday, Jan. 5, 1806

The preparations for the remains of Lord Nelson to lie in state at Greenwich Hospital having been completed, the first public exhibition of the solemn arrangement commenced this day. More than 20,000 persons were admitted, and three times that number returned disappointed. The confusion that took place on the road to Greenwich may be better conceived than described. A proper guard of Volunteers, and a great number of police officers, were stationed to preserve order. In the upper part of it a space of about sixty feet square was elevated eight steps, and inclosed by a railing, within which the body was deposited under a canopy of black velvet. The grand Painted Hall was entirely hung with black. No light from without was admitted, but lamps were distributed sufficiently to throw a ?till religious glimmer over every part of the place, while immediately in the vicinity of the coffin lofty tapers were arranged in branches, which had a very brilliant effect. Six gentlemen were seated near the coffin, in full dress, bags and swords, two at the head and four at the feet who were occasionally relieved. Several naval officers in their uniforms were also stationed round the body as mourners, and the whole area was lined by the Greenwich Volunteers, with arms reversed, &c. The great body of the hall, which approaches the elevated part, was divided by a wooden partition, placed longitudinally, and communicating with two distinct passages; by which very judicious arrangement the spectators approached the solemn scene by the Northern door, and retired through the Eastern gate. The two following days were still more crowded, and many accidents happened, from the immense pressure.—"Gentleman's Magazine," 1806.

# 1805. NELSONIANA. 1905.

## Links with Nelson :
### An Interesting Letter.

*To the Editor of* T.P.'s WEEKLY.

Dear Sir,— I see that you ask for "Links with Nelson" for your charming pages on our great hero. May I send a few ?

It may be remembered that Susannah Nelson, fourth daughter of the vicar of Burnham, married Thomas Bolton, a merchant of Wells, whose brother William was a clergyman (and by tradition a singularly jovial one when he was private chaplain at Holkham). Thomas and Susannah Bolton had two sons and four daughters, while William had two sons, William, a captain in the Navy, who was on one of Lord Nelson's ships, and Horace, a clergyman. Captain William Bolton married his first cousin, Ellen Catharine Bolton, Lord Nelson's niece, and one of the four daughters of Thomas Bolton. He was knighted, and retired to Burnham (near the ancestral Burnham Thorpe) and was the father of the "three daughters" who for generations are a tradition in the family. In the journalistic phrase,

"a pathetic interest is attached to the fact" that one of them was called Emma Horatio from Lady Hamilton, and "her devoted Nelson," as he so often signed himself. It cannot be too often repeated that while Nelson lived his enchantress was honoured and beloved by all his relatives. Sir William Bolton's third daughter married Doctor Girdlestone, son of the Reverend Henry Girdlestone, well known as Vicar of Earlham, near Norwich, and friend of the Gurney family, whose memoirs frequently refer to him. (His brother was the doctor at Wells at whose house Lady Hamilton stayed when Lord Nelson was away on foreign service.)

### *Nelson's brother-in-law.*

Lady Bolton and Sir William settled at Burnham, in Norfolk, when he left the Navy, and with them lived her twin sister and her father Thomas Bolton, as well as his brother, the Reverend William (who was both her uncle and her father-in-law). They are said to have been magnificently handsome old men, whose white hair fell in long curls, and whose features were very finely cut. I possess the portrait of one of them, and cannot but be proud to have

Nelson's brother-in-law among the silhouettes and portraits of those connected with my family. Besides her uncle and father Lady Bolton found room at her pretty home for her daughter, Eliza Girdlestone, and as many of her round dozen of children as could be packed away in the roomy old mansion. They, of course, were the great grand-nieces and nephews of Lord Nelson ; and one, Horace, doubled the family tie by marrying another Bolton. It is interesting to note how Laird Clowes endeavours to prove that Nelson's was an emphatically middle-class family, though distinctly of gentle blood. Prosperous tradesmen and Norwich manufacturers were their forbears. Fortunate farmers and well-to-do yeomen were the uncles and brothers of our hero's father, while the great Admiral's sisters were apprenticed to various trades, and one of his aunts was married to a prosperous shoemaker. Whilst laying stress on these relations, Clowes is forced to record many prebendaries, vicars, and rectors, as well as several sea captains ; but the fact remains that though the blue blood of the Walpoles flowed in his veins, young Horatio Nelson was mainly connected with the great middle-class of East Anglia. But it was a rising and a vigorous middle-class—with each generation improving on the social status of the last—and if Edmund, Rector of Sporle and Hilborough (later of Burnham) had but £80 a year, he managed— with a fine middle-class sense of rectitude—to maintain his mother and her family, and to pay off his father's just debts. Surely there was quiet heroism here ? As great, in its modest way, as was that displayed by his son Horatio at Trafalgar!

### His milliner sister.

As for Susannah, sister of Lord Nelson, with whom my few recollections (at second-hand) are chiefly connected, she was born in 1755, and "her father saw that she had a good school education," but owned that "as I could not give her a fortune equal to an independency it was most to her advantage to be placed out at some female trade." So at eighteen Susannah, sister of the future hero, was bound for three years to Messrs. Watson, "reputable milliners at Bath, where she acquitted herself with much credit and propriety." After becoming assistant in another Bath shop she inherited in 1777 a legacy from a family friend of £500, and a year later her uncle, Captain Suckling, left her £1,000. When this good fortune smiled on Susannah she gave up her business, and in 1780, being then five-and-twenty years of age, she married Mr. Thomas Bolton, a corn, malt, and coal merchant, of Wells, who, a year later, went across to Ostend, then so closely connected by mercantile ties with Norfolk. Here he became a free-burgher of the town and returned to Norwich, where he settled as a merchant in 1783. He had many children, but few of them survived. One was George, the boy who was sent to sea under his uncle, Lord Nelson, only to die there, to the bitter grief of the tender-hearted hero. Another was Thomas Bolton, who, in 1835, became the second Earl Nelson.

### His contempt for money.

Writing to his father, the great Lord Nelson said of the inheritance he had carved with his sword, " It shall go to you, my dear father, and in succession to my eldest brother and children male. William the same. Then Mr. Bolton's boys, Mrs. Matcham's (his youngest sister), and then to my nearest relations."

Again, in writing to his wife in 1799, he says :

Although I have been writing till I am nearly blind, I will not let this opportunity slip of sending a line, not to say I am contented and happy, for neither one nor other is near me ; but enough of that. I hope as soon as the East India money (£10,000) is paid that my present for my brothers and sisters will be paid. And it is my intention, if my RIGHT is allowed for the RICH Spanish frigate, to do something for Mr. Bolton and my dear sister. If I do not write to her she must not think that she is out of my thoughts, and whoever knows me knows that I despise money except as it may be useful to my friends.

Susannah Bolton's other brother, Edmund, was devoted to her also. He was the eighth son of the Burnham vicar, and after being apprenticed to a Burnham tradesman was taken as assistant by Thomas Bolton in his Ostend counting house, and was also his partner in the ownership of a trading vessel engaged in the then lucrative commerce between the Norfolk coast and the Hook of Holland. But consumption claimed him when but twenty-seven, and, dying in 1789, he left all he had to the much-loved sister, and later to her twin daughters, Catharine and Susannah. Clowes tells us that the fate of Edmund profoundly impressed Lord Nelson, who began to fancy " he, too, was in a decline," although his lungs were perfectly sound. Of the eleven children born at the old vicarage, it is interesting to note how many turned to trade: Maurice was in the excise, Susannah a milliner, William a clergyman, Ann an apprentice in a lace shop in Ludgate Street, Edmund a tradesman, and Suckling a grocer and draper. To quote Laird Clowes: " This does not disparage the vicar, who was an honourable and hard-working man, who pinched himself repeatedly to start his children in life, but it accentuates the fact that the great sea-captain had a harder task before him than is usually imagined. So long as his Uncle Suckling lived, he had interest, but he died in 1778, when Nelson was under twenty and still a lieutenant. Thus, after losing his only naval patron, he had but his own merits to push him on."

### Playing at Nelson.

It is most interesting to see how soon the family rose in the social scale. The generous bequests of Captain Suckling aided the girls, and the dearly-loved Susannah soon had a prosperous home. My " links with Nelson " start with her daughter, Lady Bolton, in whose home at Burnham a cheerful and hospitable country house, a merry young family— sons and daughters of the Doctor at Fakenham—was wont to gather, as a second home, in the early days of the last century. The pleasant old Norfolk manor was full of the belongings of the great Admiral, then but lately dead. In the attics at the top of the house were rows of sea-chests, sent home by him, and crammed with discarded uniforms, epaulets, and possessions of all sorts. In the gun-room were his fowling-pieces—long disused, but sent home by him for safe keeping. And when the young people wanted to amuse themselves by charades in the long winter evenings, Lady Bolton would hand them the keys that unlocked the old padlocks, saying, " Wear whatever you like, my dears; all the things in that attic are Lord Nelson's." My aged great-aunt, now nearly eighty-four, tells me that many and many a time she and her sisters " dressed up " in the hero's cocked hat, brandished his sword, and

buttoned themselves into the uniform that suited his slender figure far better than their buxom youthful contours. And my father-in-law, who only died three years ago at eighty-four, had been given Nelson's very own gun by Lady Bolton, and cared so little for it that he actually gave away Nelson's gun to a poacher in exchange for some tips about water-fowl or some such sporting mystery!

Later on, two of the lively girls who masqueraded in Nelson's garments married two great-nephews of the hero, and through them became the possessors of many of his belongings. amongst them two splendid flagons which they weakly lent to one of the great nautical exhibitions, and which— as some old author whose cherished tomes were filched from him says ruefully—" came not again." But to one of the sisters—long widowed—there came within the last fifteen years, incredible as it may seem, a certain sum of money from the Admiralty, which was her thirteenth or twentieth share (I don't know the exact proportion) of prize-money for one of the countless ships taken by her husband's great uncle, and only now accounted for to his representatives. And the old lady, quite unexcited by an event so historic and thrilling, calmly cashed her cheque and threw the envelope and announcement into her waste-paper basket in the most orderly manner, whereas her kinsfolk would have prized that document as far beyond price.

### Lovely Lady Hamilton.

This lady's father—the country doctor in Norfolk—who knew Nelson well, had a curious experience, and very interesting one, when he was acting as assistant to a very well-known doctor at Wells. He was Doctor Girdlestone, nearly connected with the Nelson family, and the hero had entrusted the lovely Lady Hamilton to his care during one of his absences in fighting times. The lite at Wells must have seemed triste to the vivacious young beauty, and she beguiled the time by bewitching the good-looking young doctor. In later life he related to his family how she would sit there with him, singing to him in her exquisite voice, and even dancing with some of those wonderful effects " wrought by swaying scarves and attitudes of classic grace." Lucky young doctor to fall under the fascination of the woman whose very name is still, after a hundred years, sufficient to conjure up before even the deadest imagination a vision of deathless charm! In the evening of his life he would dwell proudly on those days in the dull Norfolk village that were lit for him by such memories, and while his daughters loved to hear him, they record that their mother would sit listening in silence "with a curiously sarcastic smile on her face."

These, sir, are my few poor "links with Nelson," and I venture to record them for your delightful paper.

MARY DAMANT.

P.S.—"A link with Nelson" was sworn to in a recent case concerning the rights of public landing at Cowes, when a very old man bore witness to having gone down on the quay or hard, "with other nippers of the town" to see the great Lord Nelson land there, on his way to visit Lady Hamilton, "then staying at Corke's lodgings in the town of Cowes."

Lammas, Cowes.

## August 18, 1905.

# 1805.   NELSONIANA.   1905.

## Nelson's Valet, Tom Allen.

Nearly fifty years ago a correspondent, signing himself "F. C. H.," contributed the following memories to that wonderful storehouse, "Notes and Queries":

Lord Nelson's well-known valet, Tom Allen, lived for some time close to me, he being then retained in the service of Sir William Bolton. I met Tom almost every day in my walks, and often got into chat with him about his brave and noble master, Lord Nelson. Among other things, I spoke of his wearing his decorations at Trafalgar. Now Tom, who had been with him in so many other engagements, was by mere accident prevented from arriving in time on that last memorable occasion, having left London after his lordship, and not arriving till the battle was over, and his master's career of glory brought to a brilliant close. But it may be amusing to record Tom's opinion and observations. He said, "I never told anybody that if I had been there, Lord Nelson would not have been killed; but this I have said, and say again, that if I had been there, he should not have put on that coat. He would mind me like a child; and when I found him bent upon wearing his finery before a battle, I always prevented him. 'Tom,' he would say, 'I'll fight the battle in my best coat.' 'No, my lord, you shaun't.' 'Why not, Tom?' Why, my lord, you fight the battle first; and

then I'll dress you up in all your stars and garters, and you'll look something like.'" Thus poor old faithful Tom Allen gave himself credit for having saved his master's life by his rigid discipline in attire on former occasions; and it was evident that he was of opinion that he should have saved it once more at Trafalgar.

Tom's accounts of other memorable events of Nelson's life were given with equal naïveté. His old age was rendered comfortable in Greenwich Hospital, where he held the office of pewterer till his death.

## "Always Go At Them."

In that very fine book of naval memoirs, "The Autobiography of a Seaman," written fifty years ago by Thomas, tenth Earl of Dundonald, occurs the following noteworthy appreciation of Nelson:

"It was never my good fortune to serve under his lordship, either at that or at any subsequent period. During our stay at Palermo I had, however, opportunities of personal conversation with him, and from one of his frequent injunctions, 'Never mind manœuvres—always go at them,' I subsequently had reason to consider myself indebted for successful attacks under apparently difficult circumstances.

"The impression left on my mind during these opportunities of association with Nelson was that of his being an embodiment of dashing courage, which would not take much trouble to circumvent an enemy, but being confronted with one would regard victory so much a matter of course as hardly to deem the chance of defeat worth consideration.

"This was, in fact, the case; for though the enemy's ships were for the most part superior to ours in build, the discipline and seamanship of their crews was in that day so inferior as to leave little room for doubt of victory on our part. It was probably with the object of improving his crews that Admiral Bruix had risked a run from the Mediterranean to Brest and back, as just now detailed. Had not Lord Keith been delayed at Gibraltar, and afterwards recalled to Minorca, the disparity of numbers on our side would not have been of any great consequence.

"Trafalgar itself is an illustration of Nelson's peculiar dash. It has been remarked that Trafalgar was a rash action, and that had Nelson lost it and lived he would have been brought to a court-martial for the way in which that action was conducted. But such cavillers forget that, from previous experience, he had calculated both the nature and amount of resistance to be expected, such calculations forming as essential part of his plan of attack as even his own means for making it. The result justified his expectations of victory, which were not only well founded but certain."

## Lady Hamilton's Portraits.

It is with her introduction to Romney that the public interest of Lady Hamilton's life commences, says a writer in "Blackwood's Magazine" of 1860. He continues:

Marvellous and inscrutable are the ways by which "Providence doth shape our ends!" Had that face been less beautiful, had the heart of its possessor been less brave and faithful, had she lacked courage or promptitude—or, strange as it may sound, had she been less frail, had she possessed fewer virtues or fewer faults—the whole course of History might have been changed, and the Nile, and even Trafalgar, have had no place in the annals of England.

That Romney, like his friend Hayley, the biographer of Cowper, conceived a romantic attachment to the beautiful subject of his pencil, is abundantly shown by his letters. "The Divine Lady," as he calls her, was the object of sentimental and distant adoration, and never did devout worshipper pay more precious homage at the shrine of his idol. He painted as many as twenty-three pictures of her.

The following is a list of the pictures painted by Romney from Lady Hamilton, and given in J. Romney's Life of the Painter: 1. "Nature," 1782; 2. Circe, painted about the same time—unfinished; 3. Iphigenia; 4. St. Cecilia; 5. Bacchante—sent to Sir W. Hamilton at Naples, and lost at sea; 6. Alope; 7. The Spinstress; 8. Cassandra—Boydell's Shakespeare Gallery; 9. Three-quarters, Straw Hat, "Emma"; 10. Bacchante; 11. Half-length; 12. Do., given to her mother; 13, 14. Calypso and Magdalen—Prince of Wales; 15, 16, 17. Joan of Arc, Pythian Priestess, and Cassandra; 18. Half-length, Reading, light reflected on the face; 19. Three-quarters, 1792; 20, 21, 22. Three-quarters, side face. Two other unfinished heads.

In addition to this list, there is a very beautiful figure called The Seamstress, which was painted from Lady Hamilton. She was also the original of Reynolds's celebrated Bacchante; and of two remarkably fine full-lengths by Hoppner, The Comic Muse and A Magdalen, belonging to the Marquess of Hertford at Ragley. There is a magnificent full-length, by Lawrence, in the National Gallery of Scotland, and a very lovely chalk head by the same artist, signed "Emma," in the British Museum.

## Nelson's Funeral Car.

It is related in Sir H. Nicolas's "Despatches and Letters of Lord Nelson" that the funeral car which conveyed the remains of Lord Nelson twice underwent alteration. It was at first found to be too high to admit of its passage under the arch of Temple Bar. This mistake being remedied, it was then discovered that its width would not allow of its admission through the gates of the Admiralty!

19

## German Lines to Nelson.

I do not know what incident, beyond what may be inferred, inspired the following lines, which appeared in the "Hamburg Nachrichter" on November 2, 1800:

### AU NELSON.

Wass Kümmert dich der Diamant
Den dankbar einer Fürstin Hand,
Held Nelson, dir gegeben?
Setz' nur für den verlorenen Stein
"Aboukir" in des Degens Griff hinein,
So hast du mehr als Fürsten je gegeben.

They may be rendered as follows:

### TO NELSON.

What loss, heroic Nelson, do you fret?
Is it the diamond in your sword-hilt set,
Gift from a hand whence all were proud
   to take it?
In the sword's grip, upon the ravished
   spot,
Grave but the word "Aboukir"—and
   your lot
Is prouder than Princess's gift can
   make it!

---

## Nelson and the Apple-woman.

The following story was first given to the public by Cuthbert Bede: Nelson was passing an evening with the family of a London hosier, when the paterfamilias, coming in from the street, narrated as an amusing anecdote a misadventure which had just befallen a poor apple-woman. The poor woman had her stall in the street; a man, while pretending to purchase apples, had made fast one end of a cord to a leg of the apple-stall, and the other end to the back of a hackney coach. Off went the coach, dragging the apple-stall along with it; the fruit was scattered in the mud, the apple-woman was in tears and despair; the hosier thought it a most capital joke, and laughed immoderately. But Nelson thought it no laughing matter; his kindly heart was touched by the poor woman's distress, and he at once left the house, sought out the apple-woman, and more than recompensed her for the loss she had sustained.

## Lady Hamilton.

This is Nelson's year, and a book which I can confidently recommend to my readers is Mr. Richard H. Holmes's "Horatio Nelson" (Walter Scott. 2s. 6d. net). I quote from its pages this interesting sketch of the youth of the beautiful Lady Hamilton:

Her original name was Amy Lyon, and she had the misfortune to be born of exceedingly poor parents, beginning life uneducated and devoid of moral training. While quite a child she wandered up to London, expecting to find fortune there, and, thanks to her lovely face—for she was a beautiful child—she was ruined and became an outcast. Mr. Charles Greville, who was the nephew of Sir William Hamilton, saw the poor creature when she was seventeen years of age, and recognised not only the beauty of her face but saw there lay behind a beauty of character which might, under careful training, develop into extraordinary power. He protected her and re-named her Emma Hart and as Emma Hart she was known to the world that visited him. Impulsive by nature, and capable of a far better life, Emma loved Greville passionately and devotedly, and her life could have been passed in perfect happiness in his society. Unfortunately, however, he deemed it his duty to marry.

The Emma Hart of that day was vastly different to the Amy Lyon he had taken in charge four years before, and he feared to inform her of that determination. He therefore told her that if she would journey as far as Naples to his uncle's house, he would follow her in the course of a few weeks, being prevented by business from going with her. She fell into the trap, and when, in Naples, the truth was revealed, her grief was poignant in the extreme.

Her first step was to obtain the position of Lady Hamilton, and she made Sir William marry her. She became Lady Hamilton, and well and truly did she sustain her character. Many ladies prudishly shunned her; but gradually she made her way until she became the favourite lady of Court, and the personal friend and *confidante* of the Queen.

Her keen wit told her that the man Nelson was to become a great and mighty power in Europe, and she set herself to enslave his mind so that she would receive his reflected glory and become a power in the State, and it was therefore her hand that can be detected in the letter from her husband to the returning hero.

Lady Hamilton has been styled an adventuress, but such a term is inapt. She was only the creature of circumstances, not the maker of them, until she was taught the strict necessity for making sure of her position—a position not desired by her, but thrust upon her.

She is described as a tall woman, inclined to *embonpoint*, well-shaped in form and figure, with an exceedingly beautiful face, her head charmingly formed, small ears and white teeth, intensive and expressive blue eyes with well-defined and beautifully-shaped eyebrows, and altogether charming. Some ladies record her as almost the opposite, but from the references to her early life—a life for which birth and circumstances, not choice, was to blame—their criticism must be taken guardedly.

There is no word of immorality ever laid to her charge, and there is every possible reason to believe that the love between her and Nelson was strictly platonic.

Such was the Lady Hamilton who was searching out her softest pillows for the hero, and who had already determined to attach him to her, heart and soul, and share the reflection of the glorious halo she saw instinctively was to be his crown of reward.

**August 25, 1905.**

# 1805. NELSONIANA. 1905.

### Nelson's Birthplace.

It is particularly interesting to receive family and local memoirs of Lord Nelson. From a Norfolk reader comes the following welcome communication:—

I live within walking distance of our immortal hero's birthplace, and bear, moreover, a name intimately associated with his happiest moments. There is a beautiful two-light window dedicated to the memory of my namesake and her relative in the fine old church of Burnham Market (or Westgate), one mile and a quarter from Burnham Thorpe, bearing the following inscription:

EMMA HORATIA FOLEY.
Died February 21, 1869.
Aged 64.

On the right of this we read:
MARY ANNE BOLTON.
Died December 25, 1864.
Aged 51.

The old manor house formerly occupied by the Boltons is still standing; in fact, the "seven Burnhams" all seem to have remained. "In change, unchanged" since the days when Horatio Nelson's childish feet trod their quiet roads to the distant sea he loved so well. In the adjoining parish of Burnham Sutton is a quaint hostelry, now called "The Lord Nelson," facing the church of which, with Thorpe, Nelson's father was rector. The inn is quite 200 years old, and was originally known as The Mermaid. In the days when it bore this sign the Rev. Edmund Nelson was an occasional visitor to the little parlour behind the bar, which is still unaltered, and discussed parish news over a quiet pipe and a glass of the excellent home-brewed for which the old tavern is still famous. Later on, when Horatio had won fame for the family name, the sign was altered to The Admiral Nelson, and remained so until after the hero's death, when it was altered to the one which now swings before its hospitable entrance.

This must not be confounded with The Lord Nelson at Burnham Thorpe itself, which, when first built, was often frequented by the Admiral during the slow-moving days before the Admiralty summoned him to service. The place is just the same, except for a new tiled roof and its more recent sign, and a really excellent portrait of Nelson affixed just over the door. In earlier days it was known as The Chequers. The so-called Nelson's Brook, in which Horatio is said to have launched his fleet of paper boats in boyhood's days, still flows down the dreamy old village street, though the original rectory house where he was born is, alas! no more.

An interesting relic of the past is to be found in the studio of Councillor J. W. Beeton, of Hunstanton. This consists of an old and extremely comfortable mahogany arm-chair, originally in the possession of Nelson's father, and part of the furniture of the rectory. It is in a fair state of preservation, and the owner has been offered high prices for it, but has refused to part with so valued a link with the great Admiral. Sitting in its capacious depths one can dream brief dreams of the days long fled into the mists of years, and picture a slender, boyish figure, the small, thin face lighted with a pair of brave blue eyes, resting there after a long ramble in the lanes of the well-loved village to which his thoughts fondly turned even on the last sad and glorious day of Trafalgar.

EMMA EVELYNNE HAMILTON.

---

# Nelson and Duncan Wallace.—I.

On the 14th of February, 1797, was fought the battle of Cape St. Vincent. Nelson commanded the "Captain," which he ran between the "Santissima Trinidada," a four-decker, of 136 guns, and the "San Josef," a three-decker of 112 guns. One of Nelson's petty officers was Duncan Wallace, whose long career as a sailor is set forth very graphically in a memoir edited by Thomas Kirkup. From this book I take the following:

A circumstance occurred in this battle which reflects great credit upon Wallace for his activity and courage. In boarding the San Nicholas, as he was jumping from the poop deck to the quarter deck, he was attacked by the first lieutenant of the San Nicholas, who made a pass at him with his sword. Wallace parried off the thrust, and in striking at him he broke his sword, about six inches from the guard, by hitting it against the foremost beam on the poop deck. He was now placed in a perilous situation ; not a moment was to be lost. He therefore immediately attacked the lieutenant with hand and foot, and struck

him in the neck a furious and deadly blow, causing him to fall head-foremost against the bulwarks, and was killed. Wallace instantly seized the fallen lieutenant's sword and dashed at the foe.

This deed of activity and bravery was performed in the presence, and under the eye of Nelson, who called out, "Wallace, I'll not forget you for that." He kept his word, and Wallace was made quarter-master.

---

# Nelson and Duncan Wallace.—2.

The above was not the most remarkable encounter between Wallace and Lord Nelson. Even more striking was the conversation which passed between them at the battle of Aboukir:

At this battle Wallace was shot through the right arm by a musket ball. After the wound had been dressed by Dr. Miller, he was ordered to his hammock, but he told the doctor that he would not disgrace his country by going to his hammock for such a scratch as that, that every effective man was wanted, and he would go to his duty, and attend to it, as long as he was able.

At ten o'clock the same day Nelson heard of this circumstance and sent for Wallace, when he said, "Wallace, this is the third ship and fourth battle that I have been in with you, and to-day I will make you an officer."

Wallace said, "I thank your honour for the distinction shown to me amongst so many hundreds of men, but I respectfully decline the offered promotion ; first, in consequence that you were the cause of keeping me in the service in the year 1795, contrary to the laws of my country, and cutting me off from the means of realizing a fortune by commercial pursuits. Second: If I hold an office in the British Navy under its present discipline, I must become a tool to tyranny and oppression, which is contrary to my name, my country, and my principles ; and lastly, I have my conscience to consult, and a God to meet."

After a pause Nelson looked at me rather sternly, and said, "You are a true patriot." I replied, that it was from himself that I had copied these principles.

Nelson never again offered to promote Wallace ; calling the officers tyrants was mutinous language, for which, according to the articles of war, he might have been hung, but Nelson knew his man, and never resented it.

## His Blind Eye.

It is well known that Nelson was capable of inspired disobedience. The grand instance is his behaviour at the Battle of Copenhagen, where he served under Sir Hyde Parker. Before victory had declared itself in favour of the British, and when to retire would have been discomfiture and disgrace, Admiral Parker made the signal (No. 39) for the engagement to cease. When the signal was reported to Nelson, then walking on deck, he continued his walk, and appeared to take no notice of it. The lieutenant meeting his lordship at the next turn, asked "Whether he should repeat it?" Lord Nelson answered, "No, acknowledge it." On the officer returning to the poop, his lordship called after him, "Is No. 16 (signal for close action, which had been flying from the beginning) still hoisted?" The lieutenant answered in the affirmative. Lord Nelson said, "Mind you keep it so!" He now walked the deck considerably agitated, which was always known by his moving the stump of his right arm. After a turn or two, he said to Captain Foote in a quick manner, "Do you know what's shown on board the commander-in-chief? No. 39!" On Captain F.'s asking what that meant, Nelson answered, "Why, to leave off action. Leave off action!" he repeated. "No, never while an enemy's flag is flying." He also observed to Captain Foley, "You know, Foley, I have only one eye. I have a right to be blind sometimes." And then, with an archness peculiar to his character, putting the glass to his blind eye, he exclaimed, "I really do not see the signal."

## "A Quarter Before."

When Lord Nelson was leaving London on his last, but glorious expedition against the enemy, a quantity of cabin furniture was ordered to be sent on board his ship. He had a farewell dinner-party at his house; and the upholsterer having waited upon his lordship, with an account of the completion of the goods, he was brought into the dining-room, in a corner of which his lordship spoke with him. The upholsterer stated to his noble employer that everything was finished and packed, and would go in the waggon, from a certain inn, at six o'clock. "And you go to the inn, Mr. A., and see them off." "I shall, my lord; I shall be there punctually at six." "A quarter before six, Mr. A.," returned Lord Nelson; "be there a quarter before; to that quarter of an hour I owe everything in life."

## Lord Nelson at Birmingham.

Sir,—I note you would like to hear of any links between living people and Lord Nelson. My grandmother used to speak of having seen Nelson and Lady Hamilton at Birmingham, and what she more particularly remembered was the little incident of her ladyship taking the admiral's handkerchief out of his pocket.　　　J. BAGNALL.

Hazelwood, Solihull

## A Battle's Awful Interruption.

The blowing-up of the French man-of-war, the "Orient," is one of the unforgettable events in naval warfare, and right well it is described by Southey. Nelson, wounded in the head by a piece of langridge shot, was resting in his cabin while the battle proceeded. Southey writes:

He was now left alone; when suddenly a cry was heard on the deck that the Orient was on fire. In the confusion he found his way up, unassisted and unnoticed, and, to the astonishment of every one, appeared on the quarter-deck, where he immediately gave order that boats should be sent to the relief of the enemy.

It was soon after nine that the fire on board the Orient broke out. Brueys was dead: he had received three wounds, yet would not leave his post: a fourth cut him almost in two. He desired not to be carried below, but to be left to die upon deck. The flames soon mastered his ship. Her sides had just been painted; and the oil-jars and paint-buckets were lying on the poop. By the prodigious light of this conflagration, the situation of the two fleets could now be perceived, the colours of both being clearly distinguishable. About ten o'clock the ship blew up, with a shock which was felt to the very bottom of every vessel. Many of her officers and men jumped overboard, some clinging to the spars and pieces of wreck with which the sea was strewn, others swimming to escape from the destruction which they momently dreaded. Some were picked up by our boats; and some, even in the heat and fury of the action, were dragged into the lower ports of the nearest British ships by the British sailors. The greater part of her crew, however, stood the danger till the last, and continued to fire from the lower deck. This tremendous explosion was followed by a silence not less awful: the firing immediately ceased on both sides; and the first sound which broke the silence was the dash of her shattered masts and yards falling into the water from the vast height to which they had been exploded. It is upon record, that a battle between two armies was once broken off by an earthquake: such an event would be felt like a miracle; but no incident in war, produced by human means, has ever equalled the sublimity of this co-instantaneous pause, and all its circumstances.

# 1805. NELSONIANA. 1905.

### Nelson's "Will."

Nelson made his will just before the Battle of Trafalgar opened. Captain Blackwood and Captain Hardy came on board the Victory to witness it. This is the document which they saw Nelson sign:

October 21st, 1805. Then in sight of the combined fleets of France and Spain, distant about ten miles.

Whereas the eminent services of Emma Hamilton, widow of the Right Honourable Sir William Hamilton, have been of the greatest service to my King and my country, to my knowledge, without ever receiving any reward from either our King or country:

First, that she obtained the King of Spain's letter, in 1796, to his brother the King of Naples, acquainting him of his intention to declare war against England, from which letter the Ministry sent out orders to the then Sir John Jervis to strike a stroke, if opportunity offered, against either the arsenals of Spain or her fleets. That neither of these was done is not the fault of Lady Hamilton: the opportunity might have been offered.

Secondly, the British fleet under my command could never have returned the second time to Egypt had not Lady Hamilton's influence with the Queen of Naples caused letters to be wrote to the Governor of Syracuse that he was to encourage the fleet's being supplied with everything, should they put into any port in Sicily. We put into Syracuse, and received every supply, went to Egypt, and destroyed the French fleet.

Could I have rewarded these services, I would not now call upon my country; but as that has not been in my power, I leave Emma Hamilton, therefore, a legacy to my King and country, that they will give her an ample provision to maintain her rank in life.

I also leave to the beneficence of my country my adopted daughter, Horatia Nelson Thompson, and I desire she will use in future the name of Nelson only.

These are the only favours I ask of my King and country at this moment, when I am going to fight their battle. May God bless my King and country and all those I hold dear. My relations it is needless to mention; they will, of course, be amply provided for.

The two captains stood beside him while he wrote his name:

Nelson and Bronte,

and appended theirs—

Witnesses: Henry Blackwood.
J. M. Hardy.

Horatia was then five years old. As everyone knows, the Government ignored the hero's desires in regard to Lady Hamilton, who ended her days in poverty, and died miserably at Calais.

## If Napoleon Did!

The following intensely interesting suggestions formed part of Lord Nelson's plan for dealing with Napoleon's threatened invasion of Great Britain from Boulogne. The document was supplied by Nelson to the Admiralty:

I will suppose that forty thousand men are destined for this attack, or rather surprise of London; twenty thousand will land on the west side of Dover, sixty or seventy miles from London, and the same number on the east side: they are too knowing to let us have but one point of alarm for London. Supposing two hundred craft collected at Boulogne, &c., they are supposed equal to carry twenty thousand men. In very calm weather they might row over, supposing no impediment, in twelve hours; at the same instant by telegraph the same number of troops would be rowed out of Dunkirk, Ostend, &c. These are the two great objects to attend to from Dover and the Downs, and perhaps one of the small ports to the westward.

Boulogne (which I call the central point of the western attack) must be attended to. If it is calm when the enemy row out, all our vessels and boats appointed to watch them must get into the Channel and meet them as soon as possible; if not strong enough for the attack they must watch, and keep them company till a favourable opportunity offers. If a breeze springs up, our ships are to deal destruction; no delicacy can be observed on this occasion.

But should it remain calm, and our flotilla not fancy itself strong enough to attack the enemy on their passage, the moment they begin to touch our shore, strong or weak, our flotilla of boats must attack as much of the enemy's flotilla as they are able—say only one-half or two-thirds; it will create a most powerful diversion, for the bows of our flotilla will be opposed to their unarmed stern, and the courage of Britons will never, I believe, allow one Frenchman to leave the beach. A great number of Deal and Dover boats to be on board our vessels, off the port of Boulogne, to give notice of the direction taken by the enemy. If it is calm, vessels in the Channel can make signals of intelligence to our shores, from the North Foreland to Orfordness, and even as far as Solebay, not an improbable place, about seventy or eighty miles from London.

Whenever the enemy's flotilla can be seen our divisions are to unite, but not intermix, and to be ready to execute such orders as may be deemed necessary, or as indispensable services may require. For this purpose men of such confidence in each other should be looked for, that (as far as human foresight can go) no little jealousy may creep into any man's mind, but to be all animated with the same desire of preventing the descent of the enemy on our coasts. Stationary floating batteries are not, from any apparent advantage, to be moved, for the tide may prevent their resuming the very important stations assigned them: they are on no account to be supposed neglected, even should the enemy surround them, for they may rely on support, and reflect, that perhaps their gallant conduct may prevent the mischievous designs of the enemy.

Whatever plans may be adopted, the moment the enemy touch our coasts, be it where it may, they are to be attacked by every man afloat or on shore. This must be perfectly understood. *Never fear the event.*

---

## Nelson's Boatswain.

The relations between Nelson and his men, as I showed last week in the case of Duncan Wallace, are intensely interesting. In Mrs. Hilda Gamlin's "Nelson's Friendships," several examples of these "friendships" are given. Here is one:

Nelson's favourite boatswain was Thomas Carter, who was paid off at Portsmouth when peace was proclaimed in 1815. He hired two postchaises, and treated some of his friends to a free ride with him to his native village, Pangbourne-on-Thames, where for several days he kept open house at the Elephant and Castle Inn, engaged a band of musicians from Reading, and entertained with lavish hospitality all who were willing to accept of it, until the whole of his prize-money and accumulated pay came to an end. After enjoying a pension for some years the old hero passed peacefully away, and was buried with the Union Jack for a winding-sheet, according to his own expressed wish, in Pangbourne Churchyard.

At his funeral another flag was hoisted half-mast on a pole in front of his cottage as a mark of respect. It had a narrow escape of being torn to pieces by the villagers, who in their ignorance of emblems of mourning regarded the ensign as a sign of rejoicing at the decease of their friend.

The young people of Pangbourne loved to gather round him of an evening, and hear the old sea-stories he had to tell and his anecdotes of the great Lord Nelson. Among those interested listeners was the son of a gentleman resident at Pangbourne-on-Thames, and the desire to possess Nelsonian relics caused him to acquire all such as he found himself able to purchase, until a goodly collection of original letters became his, accumulated by degrees. The young gentleman who learnt his first lessons on the glorious career of Nelson from the old boatswain Carter is J. C. Holding, Esq., now of Southsea ; and the documents he gradually became possessed of have formed the basis of this present work on Nelson's friendships written " In Memoriam."

## Joseph Gillman.

Joseph Gillman (says the same writer) was one of the foremost mutineers at the Nore. Joe dictated the effective telegraphic message to Mr. Pitt : " Unless the demand for double pay was granted to soldiers as well as sailors, in one hour they would weigh anchor, and with fifty ships of war in four hours lay London in ashes." In this case Joe's threat conquered without blows both Minister and Monarch.

This rebellious act was Joe's chief glory, and he used to say " he had rendered no other service to his country or to man to be compared to it." He was personally selected by Lord Nelson to accompany him in the St. George to the Baltic, where twelve ships under Nelson accomplished what the forty under Admiral Parker declined. At Copenhagen Joe Gillman received a compound fracture of both legs. He served in the Royal Navy for about eighteen years, and was ever foremost in the hour of danger. He was one of the " forlorn hope " in the storming of Seringapatam, and for his many and long

services his country rewarded him with —nothing! So said the " Manchester Guardian " when old Joe died at Hulme, on June 25, 1855, aged ninety-six years.

---

## Nelson's Hunger for Victory before Trafalgar.

On September 2 (writes Mr. Clark Russell in his admirable " Life of Nelson ") Captain Henry Blackwood arrived in London with important news for the Admiralty. He had been despatched from the Irish station by Admiral Drury with instructions to trace the movements of the combined fleets under Villeneuve and Gravina, who had put to sea from Ferrol after the action with Sir Robert Calder off Finisterre. Blackwood watched them into Cadiz, then after a passage of five days arrived in England to report the fact. On his way to London he called at Merton. The hour was about five in the morning, but Nelson was already up. He instantly exclaimed to Blackwood : " I am sure you bring me news of the French and Spanish fleets, and I think I shall yet have to meet them." He followed Blackwood to London, and several times said to him when they again met, of speaking of the operations he contemplated on returning to the Mediterranean : " Depend on it, Blackwood, I shall yet give Mr. Villeneuve a drubbing."

In Harrison's " Life of Lord Nelson " this anecdote, which is unquestionably authentic, is very dramatically amplified. It is there related that Captain Blackwood's account of the enemy's fleet " was nothing to " Nelson, who exclaimed : " Let the man trudge it, who has lost his budget! " But though he said this gaily, Lady Hamilton observed that his countenance fell and wore an air of gloom. He went for a walk with her in one of the paths of Merton Garden, which he always called the quarterdeck, and she told him that she perceived he was low and uneasy. " No," he answered with a smile, " I am as happy as possible," adding, " that he saw himself surrounded by his family ; that he found his health better since he had been at Merton ; and that he would not give a sixpence to call the King his uncle." To this Lady Hamilton replied : " That she did not believe what he said, and that she would tell him what was the matter with him ; that he was longing to get at these French and Spanish fleets; that he considered them as his own property, and would be miserable if any other man than himself did the business; that he must have them, as the price and reward of his long watching, and two years' uncomfortable situation in the Mediterranean." And she finished by saying: "Nelson, however we may lament your absence, and your so speedily leaving us, offer your services, immediately, to go off to Cadiz; they will be accepted, and you will gain a quiet heart by it. You will have a glorious victory; and then you may come here, have your otium cum dignitate, and be happy." He looked at her for some moments in silence, and then, with tears in his eyes, exclaimed: "Brave Emma! Good Emma! If there were more Emmas there would be more Nelsons; you have penetrated my thoughts. I wish all you say, but was afraid to trust even myself with reflecting on the subject. However, I will go to town."

September 8, 1905.

# 1805.  NELSONIANA.  1905.

## No More Lieutenants That Way.

Nelson (says Captain Mahan, in his enthralling biography) loved to bestow promotion, when deserved, on the spot; to give a man his spurs, if it might be, on the field of battle. But vacancies would not always offer at the happy moment. A brother of Hillyar's was a midshipman in one of two boats sent to visit a suspicious vessel. A sudden and staggering fire killed the lieutenant in command, besides disabling a number of the boats' crews. The men hesitated; but the lad, left in charge, cheered them on and carried the vessel by boarding. Although he was but a couple of months over fifteen, Nelson gave him at once his commission into the vacancy made by the lieutenant. One very dark night, the Victory being under way, a midshipman, at the imminent risk of his life, leaped into the sea to save a seaman who had fallen overboard, and otherwise would have been drowned. Nelson gave him, too, his commission the following morning; but, seeing the jubilation among the young man's messmates, and thinking the act might be a dangerous precedent, he leaned over the poop and said, smiling good-naturedly, "Stop, young gentlemen! Mr. Flin has done a gallant thing to-day, and he has done many gallant things before, for which he has now got his reward. But mind, I'll have no more making lieutenants for men falling overboard."

## The Nelson Brick?

At the present time there lies in the Paston Grammar School, North Walsham, in Norfolk, carefully preserved in a glass case, a brick bearing the initials "N. H.," which, it is stated, were cut by Nelson during the time he was a scholar there. For many years this brick has been regarded with much awe and reverence by the many visitors to the school, some coming a considerable distance expressly for the purpose of viewing it. Up to just lately very little doubt has existed as to the genuineness of the initials, but it has now transpired that in all probability the brick had no connection at all with Nelson, and that the initials were the work of a mischievous schoolboy. This was made public as the outcome of a speech made by Mr. Rider Haggard at a Nelson celebration in Norfolk. Mr. Haggard stated that the brick was discovered about twenty years ago when he and his father, who was an old boy of the school, paid a visit to North Walsham. On that occasion, Mr. Haggard, senr., remarked that when he was at the school there was a brick in a wall on which Nelson had cut his name, and that he believed he could find the spot. A search was made, and the brick was found in a wall which had been partially demolished by a falling tree in a gale which raged a few days previously. Soon after Mr. Haggard made this announcement, a Norfolk gentleman,

27

who was a scholar at the school, stated he could prove Nelson had nothing whatever to do with the engraving of the initials. It seems that subsequent to a letter Mr. Haggard's father sent to the "Times," in which he said he had a belief in the existence of such a brick, a search was made for it by two of the schoolboys. This was about twenty-four years ago. The mischievous thought then entered the head of one of the boys, who came from Oswestry, to cut the initials himself and fill them with moss to make the deception the more complete. The gentleman who volunteers this information states that he, in company with others, saw it done, and that he is prepared to disclose the names of those who were present at the time should the verity of his story be questioned. When the fraudulent brick had been created, the boys announced they had made a genuine discovery, and when Mr. Haggard and his father came they were shown it. Another thing which seems to still more support this story is that it is scarcely possible, had Nelson really cut his initials, they would have survived the influence of the weather.

---

## A Painter Baffled by Nelson's Face.

One day, after tea in the drawing-room at Merton, Lord Nelson was earnestly engaged in conversation with Sir Samuel Hood. A guest observed to Sir Alexander Ball that Lord Nelson was at work, by his countenance and mouth; that he was a most extraordinary man, possessing opposite points of character: little in little things, but by far the greatest man in great things he ever saw; that he had seen him petulant in trifles, and as cool and collected as a philosopher when surrounded by dangers, in which men of common minds, with clouded countenance, would say, "Ah! what is to be done?" It was a treat to see his animated and collected countenance in the heat of action.

Sir Alexander remarked this seeming inconsistency, and mentioned that, after the Battle of the Nile, the captains of the squadron were desirous to have a good likeness of their heroic chief taken, and for that purpose employed one of the most eminent painters in Italy. The plan was to ask the painter to breakfast, and get him to begin immediately after. Breakfast being over, and no preparation being made by the painter, Sir Alexander was selected by the other captains to ask him when he intended to begin; to which the answer was, "Never." Sir Alexander said he stared, and they all stared, but the artist continued: "There is such a mixture of humility with ambition in Lord Nelson's countenance that I dare not risk the attempt."

---

## A Stern Chase.

After the Battle of the Nile Lord Nelson could not rest happy until he had captured the two French vessels, the Généreux and the Guillaume Tell, which had shown a clean pair of heels in the final confusion of that astounding fight. His opportunity came on his return to Malta. When these vessels were reported seen, and the chase began, Nelson was only anxious that the Northumberland should not beat his own flagship, the Foudroyant, in the chase. Lieutenant Parsons, in his "Nelsonian Reminiscences," admirably describes this thrilling expedition:

"Deck there!" comes the hail from Mr. Stains at the masthead. "The stranger is evidently a man-of-war. She is a line-of-battle ship, my lord, and going large on the starboard tack."

"Ah, an enemy, Mr. Stains. I pray God it may be Le Généreux. The signal for a general chase, Sir Ed'ard" (the Nelsonian pronunciation of Edward). "Make the Foudroyant fly!"

Thus spoke the heroic Nelson, and every exertion that emulation could inspire was used to crowd the squadron with canvas, the Northumberland taking the lead, with the flagship close on her quarter.

"This will not do, Sir Ed'ard. It is certainly Le Généreux, and to my flagship she can alone surrender. Sir Ed'ard, we must, and shall, beat the Northumberland."

"I will do the utmost, my lord. Get the engine to work on the sails, hang butts of water to the stays, pipe the hammocks down, and each man place shot in them, slack the stays, knock up the wedges, and give the masts play, start off the water, Mr. James, and pump the ship."

The Foudroyant is drawing ahead, and at last takes the lead in the chase.

"The Admiral is working his fin" (the stump of his right arm). "Do not cross his hawse, I advise you."

The advice was good, for at that moment Nelson opened furiously upon the quartermaster at the conn.

"I'll knock you off your perch, you rascal, if you are so inattentive. Sir Ed'ard, send your best quartermaster to the wheel."

"A strange sail ahead of the chase!" called the look-out man.

"Youngster, to the masthead. What! Going without your glass, and be d——d to you. Let me know what she is immediately."

"A sloop of war or frigate, my lord," shouted the young signal-midshipman.

"Demand her number."

"The Success, my lord."

"Captain Peard. Signal to cut off the flying enemy—great odds, though—thirty-two small guns to eighty large ones."

"The Success has hove-to athwart hawse of the Généreux, and is firing her larboard side. The Frenchman has hoisted his tricolour with a rear-admiral's flag."

"Bravo! Success. At her again."

"She has wore round, my lord, and firing her starboard broadside. It has winged her, my lord; her flying kites are blazing away all together."

The enemy is close on the Success, which must receive her tremendous broadside.

The Généreux opens her fire upon her little enemy, and every person stands aghast, afraid of the consequences. The smoke clears away, and there is the Success, crippled, it is true, but, bull-dog like, bearing up after the enemy.

"The signal for the Success to discontinue the action and come under my stern," said Lord Nelson. "She has done well for her size. Try a shot from the lower deck, Sir Ed'ard."

It goes over her.

"Beat to quarters, and fire coolly and deliberately at her masts and yards."

Le Généreux at this moment opened her fire on us, and as a shot passed through the mizzen stay-sail, Lord Nelson, patting one of the youngsters on the head, asked him jocularly how he relished the music; and observing something like alarm on his countenance, consoled him with the information that Charles XII. ran away from the first shot he heard, though afterwards he was called "The Great," and deservedly, from his bravery. "I therefore," said Lord Nelson, "hope much from you in future."

Here the Northumberland opened her fire, and down came the Tricolour amid the thunder of our united cannon.

---

## Cat and Mouse Play off Toulon.

In 1804 the watching by Nelson's ships of Latouche Treville's ships off Toulon led to an incident which made Nelson very angry. Against three British vessels eight French sail of the line came out of Toulon. Naturally the Phœbe, Amazon, and Excellent did not fight, and this led Latouche to claim the "retirement" of the British fleet. Two months later Nelson heard of this, and expressed himself in amusingly violent terms. Captain Mahan says:

As the distance between the hostile bodies was apparently from twelve to fifteen miles, the French admiral's observations may have failed to recognize that the enemy, by backing his topsails, had offered a fair challenge; else, in his report of this very commonplace occurrence, he could scarcely have used, concerning the movement of heading south, the expression, prit chasse, which, whether rendered "retired," or "retreated," or, as Nelson did, "ran away," was a misrepresentation of the facts, and heightened by the assertion that he pursued till night-fall, and next morning could not see the enemy.

Writing to Elliot four days after the affair happened, Nelson mentioned casually his view of the matter. "Monsieur Latouche came out with eight sail of the line and six frigates, cut a caper off Sepet, and went in again. I brought-to for his attack, although I did not believe anything was meant serious, but merely a gasconade."

Great was his wrath, two months later, when Latouche's statement reached him, and he found that not only no mention was made of the relative numbers, but that the offensive expression quoted had been used. "I do assure you," he wrote to the Admiralty, enclosing a copy of the day's log, "I know not what to say, except by a flat contradiction; for if my character is not established by this time for not being apt to run away, it is not worth my time to attempt to put the world right!" He might well have rested there—an imputation that might have injured an untried man could provoke only a smile when levelled at his impregnable renown; but his ruffled mind would not let him keep quiet, and in private correspondence he vented his rage in terms similar to those used of the Danish commodore after Copenhagen. "You will have seen Monsieur Latouche's letter of how he chased me and how I ran. I keep it; and, by G——d, if I take him, he shall eat it." He is a "poltroon," a "liar," and a "miscreant." It may be added that no admiral, whether a Nelson or not, could have abandoned the Excellent under the conditions.

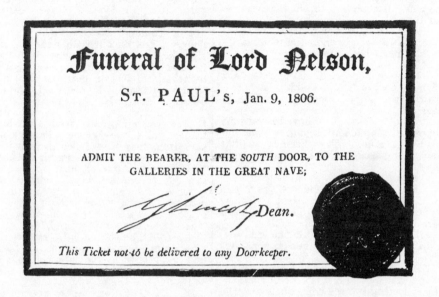

## Funeral of Lord Nelson,

### St. PAUL's, Jan. 9, 1806.

ADMIT THE BEARER, AT THE *SOUTH* DOOR, TO THE
GALLERIES IN THE GREAT NAVE;

Dean.

*This Ticket not to be delivered to any Doorkeeper.*

CARD OF ADMISSION TO ST. PAUL'S ON THE OCCASION OF NELSON'S FUNERAL.

## T. P.'s BOOKSHELF.

Readers of Jane Austen will recall her affection for the navy and the naval character, an affection largely based upon her love for her two brothers, Charles and Francis Austen, both sailors, concerning whom we have a pleasant record in "Jane Austen's Sailor Brothers" (Lane. 12s. 6d. net), by J. H. Hubback and Edith C. Hubback. The author of "Mansfield Park" was singularly free from sentiment; hers was a mind that saw too keenly below the surface of things to indulge in mere prettiness; but concerning sailors, as the writers of this book say, "she was romantic. Their very faults are lovable in her eyes, and their lives packed with interest." The naval officers in her stories are her brothers, very slightly disguised, and she was sufficient of a woman to be proud of their good looks; in a postscript to one of her letters she wrote, "Charles is in very good looks indeed." Francis Austen, early in his career, had been in touch with Nelson, but unfortunately he missed Trafalgar, his ship having been sent on convoy duty to Gibraltar. He wrote to the lady whom he subsequently married, "I never heard of his equal, nor do I expect again to see such a man." The book gives an intimate picture of the period.

# 1805.    NELSONIANA.    1905.

## Nelson's Physician on the Victory.

By the kindness of Mr. H. Nelson Hardy, of Dulwich, I am enabled to present my readers with a very interesting document—nothing less than a vivid description of life on the Victory in 1805 from the pen of the Physician to the Fleet, Dr. Gillespie. The letter I am privileged to quote was written to his sister, and is now in the possession of Mr. H. Nelson Hardy, his great-nephew.

Dr. Gillespie, as his name indicates, was of Scotch extraction, though born in the North of Ireland, and this letter was addressed to his married sister, Mrs. Hall, of Armagh.

Dr. Gillespie's name is mentioned as Physician to the Fleet in the sixth volume of "Nelson's Despatches and Letters." After the peace he lived for many years at Paris, and died among those whom he had long ceased to regard as foes on January 15, 1840, aged eighty-four years. A record of his services is inscribed on the tombstone in Père Lachaise.

On board His Majesty's ship the Victory, at sea, off the coast of Sardinia, January 7, 1805 :—

I did myself the pleasure of writing to you in great haste on the 29th ult., being at that time on board His Majesty's ship the Swiftsure, off the coast of Catalonia, on my way to join this ship, which I effected on the 2nd inst., and I am at present fully established in my office as physician to this fleet, which is (thank God) in the best possible order as to health, discipline, spirits, and disposition towards our gallant and revered commander, Lord Nelson.

### The health of the fleet.

As a proof of the state of health enjoyed by the seamen, I may instance the company of this ship, which, consisting of 840 men, contains only one man confined to his bed from sickness, and the other ships (twelve of the line), of from eighty-four to seventy-four guns, are in a similar situation as to health, although the most of them have been stationed off Toulon for upwards of twenty months, during which time very few of the men or officers (in which number is Lord Nelson) have had a foot on shore. You will perceive from this account, my dear sister, that the duties of my office are not likely at present to prove very laborious, and my duty as Inspector of the Naval Hospitals will occasion me to visit, as may be found necessary, Malta, Sicily, Gibraltar, and perhaps Naples, so that from all appearances and my experience hitherto I have no reason to be displeased with the comforts, duties, or emoluments of the office I at present fill, my salary being £465 per annum, and being situated so as to live in a princely style, free from any expense. This exemption from expense arises from my having the honour of forming one of the suite and family of Lord Nelson, whose noble frankness of manner, freedom from vain formality and pomp (so necessary to the decoration of empty little great men), can only be equalled by the unexampled glory of his naval career and the watchful and persevering diligence with which he commands this fleet. On my coming on board I found that the recommendations which my former services in the Navy had procured for me from several friends, had conciliated towards me the good opinion of his lordship and his officers, and I immediately became one of the family.

### A day on the Victory.

It may amuse you, my dear sister, to read the brief journal of a day, such as we here pass it at sea in this fine climate and in these smooth seas, on board one of the largest ships in the Navy, as she mounts 110 guns, one of which, carrying a 24lb shot, occupies a very distinguished station in my apartment.

JAN. 12.—Off the Straits of Bonifacio, a narrow arm of the sea between Corsica and Sardinia. We have been baffled in our progress towards the rendezvous of the squadron at the Madeline Islands for some days past by variable and contrary winds, but we expect to arrive at our destination to-night or to-morrow morning. To resume, my dear sister, the journal of a day : At six o'clock my servant brings a light and informs me of the hour, wind, weather, and course of the ship, when I immediately dress and generally repair to the deck, the dawn of the day at this season and latitude being apparent at about half or three-quarters of an hour past six. Breakfast is announced in the Admiral's cabin, where Lord Nelson, Rear-Admiral Murray, the Captain of the Fleet, Captain Hardy, Commander of the Victory, the chaplain, secretary, one or two officers of the ship, and your humble servant assemble and breakfast on tea, hot rolls, toast, cold tongue, &c., after which, when finished, we repair upon deck to enjoy the majestic sight of the rising sun (scarcely ever obscured by clouds in this fine climate) surmounting the smooth and placid waves of the Mediterranean, which supports the lofty and tremendous bulwarks of Britain, following in regular train their Admiral in the Victory.

### Good wines and fellowship.

Between the hours of seven and two there is plenty of time for business, study, writing, and exercise, which different occupations, together with that of occasionally visiting the hospital of the ship when required by the surgeon, I endeavour to vary in such manner as to afford me sufficient employment. At two o'clock a band of music plays till within a quarter to three, when the drum beats the tune called "The Roast Beef of Old England," to announce the Admiral's dinner, which is served up exactly at three o'clock, and which generally consists of three courses and a dessert of the choicest fruit, together with three or four of the best wines, champagne and claret not excepted ; and what exceeds the relish of the best viands and most exquisite wines, if a person does not feel himself perfectly at his ease it must be his own fault, such is the urbanity and hospitality which reign here, notwithstanding the numerous titles, the four orders of knighthood worn by Lord Nelson, and the well-earned laurels which he has acquired. Coffee and liqueurs close the dinner about half past four or five o'clock, after which the company generally walk the deck, where the band of music plays for near an hour. At six o'clock tea is announced, when the company again assemble in the Admiral's cabin, where tea is served up before seven o'clock, and as we are inclined, the party continue to converse with his lordship, who at this time generally unbends himself, although he is at all times as free from stiffness and pomp as a regard to proper dignity will admit, and is very communicative. At eight o'clock a rummer of punch, with cake or biscuit, is served up, soon after which we wish the Admiral a good-night, who is generally in bed before nine o'clock. For my own part, not having been accustomed to go to bed quite so early, I generally read an hour, or spend one with the officers of the ship, several of whom are old acquaintances, or to whom I have been known by character. Such, my dear sister, is the journal of a day at sea in fine or at least moderate weather, in which this floating castle goes through the water with the greatest imaginable steadiness, and I have not yet been long enough on board to experience bad weather.

---

# The Boatswain Who Could Not Pipe.

A thorough seaman himself (writes one of Nelson's earliest biographers), nursed in the lap of hardship, Nelson knew how to adapt his behaviour to those he commanded, and never did an officer possess their affections in a higher degree. To this love and affection he was not only indebted for his early successes, but even for his life, for there was scarcely one of his crew who would not have sacrificed himself to save his commander. A striking instance of how much he was adored by his men occurred during the last fatal conflict off Trafalgar. A seaman of the Victory was under the hands of the surgeon, suffering the amputation of an arm. "Well," said he, "this by some would be considered a misfortune ; but I shall be proud of it, as I shall resemble the more our brave commander-in-chief." Before the operation was finished tidings were brought below that Lord Nelson was shot ; the man, who had never shrunk from the pain he endured, started from his seat, and exclaimed, "Great God! I would rather the shot had taken off my head, and spared his life."

Another generous instance of the same nature was soon after evinced on board the Brilliant frigate. Being on a cruise, she fell in with several vessels, which acquainted the crew with the defeat of the combined fleet, and the death of Lord Nelson. A concern, the most general and sincere, pervaded the ship's company. While it was yet the subject of conversation, a boatswain's mate, who was then doing duty as boatswain, was ordered to pipe all hands to quarters; he did not do it readily, and the lieutenant on duty went to inquire the cause, with orders to pipe instantly. The honest fellow, after several attempts, began to sob bitterly, and said, "Hang me if I can do it; poor, dear fellow, that I have been in many a hard day with, and to lose him now. I wouldn't have cared if it had been my old father, brother, or sisters, if there were fifty more of them; but I can't think of parting with Nelson." And he went below immediately.

---

## "Bon John."

I have quoted Southey's vivid description of the blowing up of the French Orient at the Battle of the Nile. Even that awful hour had its own humours. Mr. Clark Russell writes: Shortly after ten the great ship blew up. The explosion was that of an earthquake. The concussion swept through every seam, timber, and joint of the nearest ship, with the sensation as though the solid fabrics were crumbling into staves under the feet of the seamen. The air was filled with blazing masses of rigging and timber, shot to an immense height, descending in gigantic javelins of flame and piercing the water with the hissing as of an electric storm of hail followed by blinding clouds of steam. The sight was blackened as by a lightning stroke, and the instant the prodigious glare of the explosion had passed, the darkness of the night seemed to roll down in folds of ink upon the vision of the seamen. All was hushed; every man in both fleets appeared paralysed; and for nearly a quarter of an hour it is said no gun was fired, no movement was perceptible.

From the deck of the Leander a number of the survivors of the miserable crowds which had filled the decks and 'tween decks of L'Orient were observed to be swimming towards the frigate. "The piercing cries of these unfortunate men," wrote one who was present, "seem still to vibrate on my ear, as some of them, approaching near the Leander, cried out: 'Bon John, give rop-e! Oh, bon John, give rop-e, give rop-e!' As many of them as possible we rescued from a watery grave, though

some of them, after all our endeavours, sunk to rise no more. It was wonderful to observe, notwithstanding the deplorable circumstances in which these poor fellows were placed, what strength the amor patriæ, or reluctance to acknowledge defeat, exerted in them. To one of these forlorn creatures, drenched with water and exhausted with fatigue, I said: 'Well, monsieur, what think you now of your Bonaparte?' To which the hapless man, summoning the little energy which remained in him, replied: 'Oh, Monsieur John Bull, dis nothing, dis nothing; vive Napoléon!'"

33

# 1805.　NELSONIANA.　1905.

## Nelson's Last Signal: Its Doubtful Reception.

It may not be generally known (writes Mr. S. M. Ellis, of Southwold) that Nelson's famous signal before Trafalgar, "England expects every man to do his duty," was at first rather misunderstood by his sailors, and caused some discontent and criticism amongst them.

Mr. Ellis's grandfather, General Sir S. B. Ellis, K.C.B., was engaged in the battle of Trafalgar as a lieutenant of Marines on board H.M.S. Ajax, and it fell to him to announce the Admiral's signal to the men before the action commenced. He describes this incident and his impressions of Trafalgar in his "Memoirs" as follows:—

"The Ajax returned to Plymouth to refit, and again sailed to join Lord Nelson's fleet off Cadiz, where I was engaged in the battle of Trafalgar, the 21st of October, 1805. This glorious battle, which so greatly influenced the affairs of Europe, and gave to England the supremacy of the seas, was one through which our ship passed with but little loss. There was scarcely any wind at the time, and we approached the enemy at not more than a knot and a half an hour. As we neared the French fleet I was sent below with orders, and was much struck with the preparations made by the bluejackets, the majority of whom were stripped to the waist, a handkerchief was bound tightly round their heads and over the ears, to deaden the noise of the cannon, many men being deaf for days after an action. The men were variously occupied.

Some were sharpening their cutlasses, others polishing the guns, as though an inspection were about to take place instead of a mortal combat, whilst three or four, as if in mere bravado, were dancing a hornpipe; but all seemed deeply anxious to come to close quarters with the enemy. Occasionally they would look out of the ports and speculate as to the various ships of the enemy, many of which had been on former occasions engaged by our vessels. It was at this time that Nelson's famous signal, 'England expects every man to do his duty,' was hoisted at the masthead of the Admiral's ship. These words were requested to be delivered to the men, and I was desired to inform those on the main deck of the Admiral's signal. Upon acquainting one of the quartermasters of the order, he assembled the men with: 'Avast there, lads, come and hear the Admiral's words.' When the men were mustered, I delivered, with becoming dignity, the sentence, rather anticipating that the effect on the men would be to awe them by its grandeur. Jack, however, did not appreciate it, for there were murmurs from some, whilst others, in an audible whisper, muttered, 'Do our duty! Of course we'll do our duty. I've always done mine, haven't you? Let us come alongside of 'em and we'll soon show whether we will do our duty.' Still, the men cheered vociferously, more, I believe, from love and admiration of their Admiral and leaders than from a full appreciation of this well-known signal."

---

## Lord Nelson's Prayer before Trafalgar.

The following was the entry made by the immortal Nelson in his own diary under the fatal date of October 21st, 1805, before going into action at Trafalgar:—"At daybreak saw the enemy's combined fleet from E. to E.S.E.; bore away; made the signal for order of sailing, and to prepare for battle; the enemy with their heads to the southward—at seven, the enemy wearing in succession. May the great God whom I worship grant to my country, and for the benefit of Europe in general, a great and glorious victory! And may no misconduct in anyone tarnish it! and may humanity after victory be the predominant feature in the British fleet! For myself, individually, I commit my life to Him who made me; and may His blessing light on my endeavours for serving my King and country faithfully! To Him I resign myself, and the just cause which is entrusted to me to defend.—Amen."

## Nelson and the Turbot: a Dogger Bank Incident.

Before the Battle of Copenhagen Lord Nelson was sent out second in command under Sir Hyde Parker—a timid, inefficient admiral, with whom Nelson did not, as may be imagined, get on very well. On passing the Dogger Bank he remarked that he had heard that turbots could sometimes be caught there. He then at once told a sailor to fish for one. After some time the man returned with a very fine one, when Nelson ordered it to be taken immediately in a small boat to Sir Hyde. On somebody remarking on the danger of sending a small boat in such weather, he replied, "It shall be sent. I know Sir Hyde is fond of good living, and he shall have the turbot." It was sent, and Sir Hyde wrote a letter of thanks, and came the next day to see Nelson and consult him about the coming battle. Thus was the Battle of Copenhagen won by a turbot!

Some time after, when Nelson was staying in London with a friend, Mr. Layman (who was present) was telling the story of the turbot, when his lordship remarked, "What were you saying?" "About the turbot," answered Layman. "I well remember your Lordship's great desire to catch a turbot and your surprising many by your insisting on sending it to Sir Hyde Parker, and that it so pleased him that he consented to consult you about the coming battle." His lordship smiled and replied, "You are quite right."

## The Pronunciation of Trafalgar.

One of the first literary tributes to Nelson's fame was a poem by George Canning, whose metre required the ordinary pronunciation of the name of Nelson's last victory, Tra*f*algar.

With reference to this word there is the following amusing anecdote:

Dr. Scott was one day dining at Fife House in company with Mr. Canning, when the latter very mysteriously let him into the secret (which he so cautiously divulged to the rest of the company before the evening was over) that a poem by himself was to be published next day, in which the grand naval triumph would be celebrated. He repeated some lines for Scott's opinion, who immediately found fault with the accent being thrown on the middle syllable, instead of on the last, in the word Trafalgar. Mr. Canning defended his pronunciation by the example of Gibraltar. Such a discussion as this Scott loved to his heart, and gave his opponent the pronunciation of Gibral*tar* with the most delicate precision, informing him that it was only an English corruption which miscalled that word as it was generally spoken. So for the future we must talk of Gibral*tar* and Trafal*gar*, a somewhat difficult task after so many years' use of the other accent.

The poem represents Napoleon as rejoicing over the defeat of the Austrian armies, and the capitulation of Ulm, and then shows how, in "an insolence of power,"

O'er England's seas his new dominion
    plann'd—
Whilst the red bolt yet flamed in Nelson's
    hand;
That had, which erst by Nile's affrighted
    tide,
Smote with dread fire the godless warrior's
    pride,
And strewed his flaming wrecks on Egypt's
    shore—
Exhausted Europe by the distant roar.
Roused from her trance, her shattered force
    combined,
And half redeemed the freedom of mankind.

   .    .    .    .    .    .

O price, his conquering country grieved to
    pay,
O dear-bought glories of Trafalgar's day.

## Links with Nelson.

Mr. Charles E. Hodson writes to me from far-off Mexico:

"On Sunday, the 30th of May, 1875, as the Arctic ships Alert and Discovery were passing Plymouth, Sir Harry Keppel, the Port Admiral, came out in his tender, the Princess Alice, to visit the ships, and lunched with his nephew, the Captain of the Discovery. Amongst the Admiral's entourage of antediluvians was an enthusiastic gentleman who promenaded the deck with me describing Nelson's funeral, at which he had been on duty as a midshipman. Had we run into Plymouth on our return I should certainly have accepted his pressing invitation to pay him a visit, but I never learned how long he survived."

Mr. Henry J. Liggins (Ealing) sends me another interesting link, as follows:

"In 1865 I was intimate with an old lady, Mrs. Hanrott, the widow of an eminent solicitor, who informed me she had danced with his lordship on board H.M.S. Victory.

"In 1871 I became acquainted with a Mrs. Wyner Aubrey, who, when a bride in Bruxelles, danced with the Duke of Wellington at the Duchess of Hamilton's ball before Waterloo."

## Nelson Relics in South Africa.

A. B. writes:

"Seeing the interesting letter from a correspondent at Cowes, in your issue of August 11, reminds me that several years ago I came across some Nelson relics in Greater Britain. They were in the South African home of a relation of the Dr. Girdlestone, of Wells, mentioned in that letter, and consisted of part of the Royal Standard of the Victory—the Irish quarter. It was curious to see part of the flag that had once borne 'the battle and the breeze' on one of the most famous battleships England has ever known 'draped' in a far-away Colonial drawing-room, and to think if that flag had not been victorious the fate of that Colony might have been very different. The other things were the little sea-chest, old and battered and worn, that the great Admiral had taken to sea as a middy, unwitting of the struggles and fame that awaited him; and various dishes and pieces of plate bearing the crest of Nelson and Brontë, symbols of that fame and success which crowned his gallant career."

## Nelson and Burnham Thorpe.

Nelson's father, the Rev. Edmund Nelson, M.A., was rector of the parish for almost half-a-century (A.D. 1755—1802). Horatio, his fifth son, was born at the Rectory on Michaelmas Day, 1758. His childhood was passed in Burnham Thorpe; the family was closely identified with the life of the village; his brothers served as his father's curates; his sister married Mr. Thomas Bolton, a member of a local family. The parish register contains the boy's signature, more than once, as a witness at marriages in 1769 and 1770, when he was about eleven years old. In 1770 he went to sea, and it is striking to note with what constant affection he always speaks of his Norfolk home. When afloat, he sent gifts for the relief of its distress; when ashore, he hastened thither first. Here he spent the five years—November, 1787, to January, 1793—during which he was unemployed.

In 1798, when raised to the peerage, he was created Baron Nelson of the Nile and of Burnham Thorpe, and in 1801 Viscount Nelson of the Nile and of Burnham Thorpe. On May 11, 1804, he writes touchingly, "Most probably I shall never see dear, dear Burnham again; but I have satisfaction in thinking that my bones will probably be laid with my father's, in the village which gave me birth. The thought of former days brings all my mother into my heart which shows itself in my eyes." (Page 381, "Nelson," by G. L. Browne, Esq.) His brother William, writing the Admiralty in 1806 as to the place of a memorial, when interest in the subject was high, says: "I well knew the affection he had for the place of his birth, and I truly believe, could he look out of his grave, he would say, Burnham Thorpe." (Nicholas's "Despatches of Lord Nelson," foot-note, Vol. vii., January 23, 1806.) And his well-known words to Captain Hardy, as he lay dying in the cockpit of the Victory, on the day of the battle of the "Trafalgar," 1805, "Don't throw me overboard, I wish to be buried by the side of my father and mother, unless it should please the King to order otherwise," show how his love to the village lasted to the very end. It did please the King to "order otherwise," and Nelson lies in St. Paul's Cathedral; but surely Burnham Thorpe may claim a National Memorial of her son? At present no stone or monument, or record whatever, stands here to perpetuate the memory of one of the most favourite of English heroes. It should also be noted that the title, after descending to his brothers, passed into the family of his sister, wife of Thomas Bolton, Esq., whose tomb is in All Saints' Churchyard; so that the family which now represents Nelson's services to the nation is one truly belonging to "Burnham Thorpe."

[I take the above particulars from an interesting circular just issued by the rector and churchwardens of Burnham Thorpe, where there has long been a Nelson Memorial movement to restore the church and build a Nelson Hall. Only half the original scheme has been carried out at a cost of £5,000. The like sum is now needed to complete the work, and donations, however small, will be gladly received by the Rector, the Rev. H. M. Eliott-Drake Briscoe, at Burnham Thorpe, Norfolk.]

# 1805. NELSONIANA. 1905.

## "I Hold Myself Ready."

I have received from the publishing office of the Navy League (Victoria Street, Westminster) a very interesting study of Lord Nelson by Admiral the Hon. Sir E. R. Fremantle. The author thus describes the month which Nelson spent at Merton before his memorable departure to meet Villeneuve's fleet at Trafalgar:

Nelson's life at Merton at this time was extremely happy, and though it lasted rather less than a month it was only during these few weeks that he could be said to feel any reward for his brilliant services in the ungrudging appreciation of his countrymen.

He is said to have seldom gone to London, but he visited the Admiralty, the Colonial Office, then also the War Office, and the Foreign Office, being well received, while his advice was eagerly listened to. "I am now set up for a conjurer," he writes to Keats, "and God knows they will very soon find out I am far from being one . . . but this I mentioned without fear, that if Calder," who had again been detached with eighteen sail from the Channel Fleet, "got close alongside their twenty-seven or twenty-eight sail, that by the time the enemy had beat our fleet soundly, they would do us no harm this year." Mahan here remarks on Nelson's "realisation of the possible fruitfulness of a defeat" under certain circumstances, combined with his readiness to "wait till they give me an opportunity too tempting to be resisted or till they draw near the shores of Europe." "In such qualification is to be seen the highest order of ability. This union of desperate energy with calculating wariness was in him not so much a matter of reasoning, though reason fully endorses it, as it was a gift of nature—genius, in short."

It was at this time that Nelson and Wellington met, as is believed, for the only time, of which the Duke gave the graphic account which has been often quoted.

His reception by the public was even more remarkable. "He was received in town almost as a conqueror," wrote Radstock, "and was followed round by the people with huzzas. So much for a great and good name, most nobly and deservedly acquired." "I met Nelson in a mob in Piccadilly," wrote Minto at the same time; "It is really quite affecting to see the love and respect of the whole world." In Mahan's words, "In these few days was concentrated the outward reward of a life spent in the service of his country. During them, Nelson was conspicuously the first man in England—first alike in the love of the people and in importance to the State."

It was understood from the first that he was to return to the Mediterranean, after a short rest, probably in October, but there was much anxiety about Villeneuve's Fleet, which had sailed from Corunna, and might be doing much mischief to our trade, or might be next heard of either off Brest or in the Mediterranean, and all eyes looked to Nelson. "Mr. Pitt," he tells a friend as early as the 29th, "is pleased to think my services may be wanted. I hope Calder's victory, which I am most anxiously expecting, will render my going forth unnecessary," but he writes "I hold myself ready."

## A French Account of the Battle of the Nile.

Nelson's victory in Aboukir Bay practically made Napoleon's army prisoners in Egypt. Many of the letters and despatches from this army were intercepted by the British fleet, and eventually published. One of these letters from "B. Julien François to the Female Citizen Le Blanc" (his wife), contains a description of the Battle of the Nile as viewed by the writer from Alexandria.

Noon, August 1.—Fourteen English vessels are this moment hove in sight. We make them to be twelve sail of the line and two frigates; these last came within cannon shot of Alexandria, but on ascertaining that our fleet was not in the harbour they stood off again immediately, and, with the rest of the ships, are now making with a press of sail for Aboukir, a port about three leagues from this city, where the French fleet is at anchor, strongly moored, as they say here, and in a situation to give the English a good reception.

Five o'Clock.—We discern the English fleet very clearly through our glasses. It seems about to drop anchor at Aboukir for the purpose of attacking us.

Half after Five.—The cannonade begins, and about six increases.

Seven.—It is now night, and the firing still increases.

Half after Seven.—The whole horizon seems in flames; this shows that a ship is on fire.

Eight.—The cannonade slackens a little.

Nine.—The flames augment.

A Little after Nine.—The vessel blows up! How tremendously beautiful! A sky covered with fire!

Half after Nine.—The cannonade slackens, and a thousand sailors are despatched to Aboukir by land.

Ten.—The moon rises on the right of the spot where the explosion took place. The French here are all under arms. We are assembled at the house of General Kleber, and on the terraces. Fresh detachments are hourly despatched to Aboukir to reinforce the crews of our ships.

Midnight.—The firing, which has never totally ceased, recommences with double fury. It is evident that the English are determined to sink or be sunk. We burn to know what has happened, but we shall be kept in suspense till nine in the morning.

Three o'Clock.—The firing increases in violence. It has now continued an hour.

Six.—The firing still increases; more sailors and cannoneers are sending off. It is now eight, and the firing is as brisk as ever.

Noon.—The express is arrived from Aboukir. O fatal night! O fatal action for the honour of France! The fleet is destroyed. Of thirteen sail of the line and four frigates, two only of each have made their escape. They are sailed for France, to carry you, I imagine, this dreadful news.

The writer goes on to say that Alexandria is quite safe, his wife need not be alarmed, as "the enemy are only formidable through the ignorance of our marine. Imagine our fleet in a position which allowed the English to fight them three or four to one! A piece of stupidity like this could not escape an enemy who has made the sea his peculiar element."

## Nelson's Strategy at Trafalgar.

The following is taken from Pellew's Life of Lord Sidmouth (Vol. ii., pp. 380-2):

He (Lord Sidmouth) was accustomed in after years to relate that, amongst other things, Nelson explained to him, with his finger on the little study-table, the manner in which, should he be so fortunate as to meet the combined fleets, he proposed to attack him. "Rodney broke the line in one point; I will break it in two." "There," said Lord Sidmouth to Miss Halsted, who has reported the anecdote, "is the table on which he drew the Battle of Trafalgar but five weeks before his death. It is strange that I should have used this valued relic for about thirty years without once having thought of recording on it a fact so interesting. Now," pointing to a brass plate inserted in the centre of the table, "I have perpetuated it by this brief record:

"On this 10th day of September, 1805, Vice-Admiral Lord Viscount Nelson described to Lord Sidmouth, upon this table, the manner in which he intended to engage the combined fleets of France and Spain, which he expected shortly to meet. He stated he would attack them in two lines, led by himself and Admiral Collingwood, and felt confident that he should capture either their van and centre, or their centre and rear. This he successfully effected on the 21st day of October following, in the glorious victory of Trafalgar."

## "Glasgow to Nelson."

When Sir John Carr was in Glasgow, about the year 1807, he was asked by the magistrates to give his advice concerning the inscription to be placed on the Nelson monument, then just completed. Sir John recommended as a brief and appropriate epigraph:

"Glasgow to Nelson."

"Just so," said one of the Glasgow bailies, "and as the toon o' Nelson (Neilston) is close at hand, might we not just say, 'Glasgow to Nelson sax miles'? and so it might serve for a monument and a milestone too."

## An Incident at Trafalgar.

The following incident is reported by Nelson's French (and very impartial) biographer, Jurien de la Gravière, as happening at the moment when the Victory was advancing towards the Santissima Trinidad and the Bucentaure.

Villeneuve at this moment seized the eagle belonging to his ship and displayed it to the sailors who surrounded him. 'My friends,' he exclaimed, 'I am going to throw it on board the English ship; we will follow and recover it, or perish in the attempt.' Our sailors answered these noble words with loud acclamations. Full of hope for the issue of a combat hand to hand, Villeneuve, before the smoke had shrouded the Bucentaure from the view of the squadron, addressed this last signal to his ships: 'Every ship not in action is out of her station, and must take any position which shall more quickly bring her under fire.' His duty as an admiral was terminated, it only remained for him to prove himself the bravest captain in his fleet.

October 6, 1905.

# 1805.  NELSONIANA.  1905.

## The Man Who Claimed to Have Shot Nelson.

Robert Guillemard, the French sergeant, whose "Memoirs" were published by Colburn in 1827, claimed to have shot Nelson from the tops of the Redoubtable. Great doubt rests on his narrative, but it is as follows:

In the evening English long-boats came to take away the remainder of our crew, to be divided among the vessels of the fleet, and I was taken on board the Victory. There I learned the death of Nelson: he had been wounded on the right shoulder by a ball, which penetrated obliquely and broke the spine of the back. When taken to the cockpit he ordered his surgeon, Mr. Betty, to inform him of his situation without concealment or ceremony. He learned, without the least emotion or regret, that he had only an hour to live, called for his captain (Captain Hardy), and after inquiring about the situation of the two fleets, expressly forbade him to let the English fleet know of his death, and directed the vessels to be brought to anchor as soon as the action was over on the very spot where it was fought. Captain Hardy promised to obey his orders implicitly, but he did not like to assume the responsibility. He made signs that the Admiral was dead, when Lord Collingwood took the command, and did not judge proper to come to anchor, which, perhaps, might have been dangerous on account of the gale that came on that night.

The death of Nelson was regarded by the English as a public calamity, the bitterness of which could not be allayed by the victory they had obtained. The sailors deplored him as a father, the officers as a commander, whose talents had caused the glory and prosperity of their country, and whose place would not for a long period be filled with an Admiral of equal merit. He whose loss is regretted by an entire nation—he whose death is deplored by old sailors, usually little susceptible of sentiments of attachment—should necessarily inspire some interest, even in an enemy; hence, as a man, I could not help sharing in some degree the affliction that prevailed on board the Victory, while, as a Frenchman, I had reason to rejoice at an event that had delivered my country from one of her most dangerous enemies. At any rate, from the moment in which he received his wound, and the position of the wound itself, I could not doubt for a moment that I was the author, and I have ever since been fully convinced of it. But though the shot that had brought down this Admiral had rendered a service to my country, I was far from considering it as an action of which I had a right to boast. Besides, in the general confusion, everyone could claim the honour. I might not be believed; so that I was afraid of furnishing my companions with a subject of ridicule, and did not think proper to mention it to them, nor to the French officers I saw on board the Victory. It

39

was in this manner that more than once in the course of my life carelessness and false shame have deprived me of advantages I might justly have claimed.

## Nelson's Trafalgar Signal.

Captain Blackwood, who commanded the Euryalus, but was on board the Victory, was the first man to have knowledge of Nelson's great signal. He says :

I was walking with him (Lord Nelson) on the poop, when he said, " I'll now amuse the fleet with a signal " ; and he asked me " if I did not think there was one yet wanting? " I answered that I thought the fleet seemed very clearly to understand what they were about, and to vie with each other who should first get nearest to the Victory or Royal Sovereign (Vice-Admiral Collingwood). These words were scarcely uttered when his last well-known signal was made, " England expects every man will do his duty." The shout with which it was received throughout the fleet was truly sublime. " Now," said Lord Nelson, " I can do no more. We must trust to the great Disposer of all events, and the justice of our cause. I thank God for this great opportunity of doing my duty."

## The Wording of the Signal.

The above account omits some interesting circumstances mentioned by other witnesses. Instead of setting these forth seriatim, I will quote the summary of them all which Captain Mahan makes in his brilliant Life of Nelson. This great naval writer says :

Nelson mused for a little while, as one who phrases a thought in his own mind before uttering it, and then said, " Suppose we telegraph ' Nelson confides that every man will do his duty.' " In this form it was the call of the leader to the followers, the personal appeal of one who trusts to those in whom he trusts, a feeling particularly characteristic of the speaker, whose strong hold over others lay above all in the transparent and unswerving faith he showed in their loyal support ; and to arouse it now in full force he used the watchword " duty," sure that the chord it struck in him would find its quick response in every man of the same blood. The officer to whom the remark was made

suggested " England " instead of " Nelson." To the fleet it could have made no difference—to them the two names meant the same thing : but Nelson accepted the change with delight. " Mr. Pasco," he called to the signal officer, " I wish to say to the fleet, ' England confides that every man will do his duty ' " ; and he added, " You must be quick, for I have one more to make, which is for close action." This remark shows that the columns, and particularly Collingwood's ship, were already nearing the enemy. Pasco answered, " If your lordship will permit me to substitute ' expects ' for ' confides ' it will be sooner completed, because ' expects ' is in the vocabulary, and ' confides ' must be spelt." Nelson replied hastily, but apparently satisfied, " That will do, Pasco, make it directly " ; but the slightly mandatory " expects " is less representative of the author of this renowned sentence than the cordial and sympathetic " confides." It is " Allez " rather than " Allons " ; yet even so, become now the voice of the distant motherland, it carries with it the shade of reverence, as well as of patriotism, which patriotism exacts.

## Links with Nelson.

My valued correspondent, " Thormanby," writes :

In 1872 I lectured at the Chelsea Vestry Hall on " Our Empire of the Sea," and my chairman was an old naval captain who had been a midshipman on board the Victory at Trafalgar. His name, I think, was Rowsell, but at this distance of time I cannot be sure on that point. He told me that he was standing just behind Nelson when the hero received his mortal wound, that he helped to raise him, and that the sleeve of his jacket was wet with Nelson's blood. This fine old sailor was then eighty-three—he would, therefore, have been about sixteen at the date of Trafalgar. I have never seen any man of his years so extraordinarily active and vigorous.

On a later occasion, when I delivered the same lecture at Newcastle-on-Tyne, my chairman was a Danish gentleman whose father had fought against Nelson at Copenhagen, and was an officer on the ship which Nelson boarded to demand the surrender of the crippled Danish seventy-four, Zealand.

Another link with Nelson I came across in the Isle of Man. The father of the late Deemster Stephen, whom I knew, was quarter-master on the Victory, and caught Nelson in his arms as he fell. It was he, I believe, who marked down the rifleman of the Rédoubtable, the firer of the fatal shot, and directed the aim of the two midshipmen who avenged Nelson's death by shooting the man who killed him. I was at school, and afterwards at Cambridge, with the Deemster's son, Major R. S. Stephen, sometime Mayor of Douglas, who possessed some interesting relics of his grandfather and the old Victory.

It was in the Isle of Man, too, that I met "The Man who Shot Nelson"! In those days all the lunatics of the island were confined in Castle Rushen—more like caged wild beasts than human beings. Among them was a man possessed with the hallucination that he had shot Nelson, and was suffering the just punishment for that unpardonable crime. He was a tall, powerful fellow, with a singularly mild, vacuous expression of face, and when questioned he gave a most circumstantial account of the appalling accident by which, he averred, Nelson had met death from his hand. He was a Marine, he said, on board the Victory, and, when raising his musket to fire at the Frenchmen, he pulled the trigger too soon, and the bullet hit Nelson in the breast. As he reached the climax of his story his placid features took on a look of horror, and his voice fell almost to a whisper, for the imaginary tragedy which his crazed brain had conjured up was evidently to him an awful reality—a deed not to be expiated—which put him outside the pale of human sympathy or forgiveness. As a matter of fact, the man was not born till ten years after Trafalgar; but his father had fought as a Marine on the Victory. He himself had served in the Navy, and his poor crazy fancy had woven this extraordinary fiction out of what he had heard his father tell of the battle.

## Nelson in Fiction.

In "Notes and Queries" of January 28, 1905, Mr. Jonathan Neild supplied the following interesting list of novels and tales dealing, directly or indirectly, with Nelson and his times:

G. A. Henty, "By Conduct and Courage."
Edgar Pickering, "In Press Gang Days."
G. A. Henty, "At Aboukir and Acre."
C. H. Eden, "Afloat with Nelson."
Douglas Sladen, "The Admiral."
Roland B. Molineux, "The Vice-Admiral of the Blue."
Bernard Capes, "The Extraordinary Confessions of Diana Please."
Amyot Sagon, "When George III. was King."
Horace G. Hutchinson, "A Friend of Nelson."
R. D. Blackmore, "Springhaven."
B. Perez Galdos, "Trafalgar."
Frederick Harrison, "England Expects."
Costello, "Nelson's Yankee Boy."
F. H. Winder, "With the Sea Kings."
Walter Besant and James Rice, "'Twas in Trafalgar's Bay."
W. H. Fitchett, "The Commander of the Hirondelle."
Gordon Stables, "Chris Cunningham."
Gordon Stables, "Hearts of Oak."
H. S. Huntingdon, "His Majesty's Sloop Diamond Rock."
Miss Manning, "Diana's Crescent."
Captain F. Chamier, "Ben Brace."
Captain Marryat, "Frank Mildmay."
Captain Marryat, "King's Own."
Captain Marryat, "Mr. Midshipman Easy."
W. H. G. Kingston, "The Fire Ships."
W. H. G. Kingston, "Ben Burton."
H. Collingwood, "The Log of a Privateersman."
H. Collingwood, "Under the Meteor Flag."
W. Clark Russell, "The Death Ship."
G. Manville Fenn, "Uncle Bart."
Gordon Stables, "As we Sweep Through the Deep."

## Forewarned of Death.

Nelson had a narrow escape early in the great action of October 21. While the Victory was approaching the allies' line of battle her mizen top-mast was shot away, and the wheel was shivered. Several marines fell on the poop, and Nelson gave the officer an order to disperse his men so that there might be less loss from any one shot.

"Presently a shot, that had come through a thickness of four hammocks, struck the forebrace bits on the quarter-deck, and passed between Lord Nelson and Captain Hardy." It was—says one writer—the avant-coureur of death, the death that was soon to plunge the family of England into one common grief. "They both," says Dr. Beatty, "instantly stopped, and were observed by the officers on deck to survey each other with inquiring looks, each supposing the other to be wounded. His lordship then smiled, and said, 'This is too warm work, Hardy, to last long'; and declared that, through all the battles he had been in, he had never witnessed more cool courage than was displayed by the Victory's crew on this occasion." . . . "While listening with characteristic avidity to the deafening crash made by their shot in the French ship's hull, the British crew were nearly suffocated with clouds of black smoke that entered the Victory's port-holes; and Lord Nelson, Captain Hardy, and others. that were walking the quarter-deck, had their clothes covered with the dust which issued from the crumbled woodwork of the Bucentaure's stern."

The centenary edition of Mr. Douglas Sladen's "The Admiral," just published by Messrs. Pearson at sixpence, has upon the cover a reproduction of an interesting portrait of Nelson, said to be by Rowlandson. It is taken from a rare colour print published by Tegg in 1807, and I understand that the only other known copy is in the British Museum, and that is only half coloured. It seems curious that a portrait of a popular hero, which one would imagine to have had a large sale, should have become rare so soon. By the way, Messrs. Treherne are to publish shortly another book by Mr. Douglas Sladen and Miss Norma Lorimer, called "Queer Things About Sicily."

October 13, 1905.

# 1805.   NELSONIANA.   1905.

## The Heroic Figure.

From a newly-published book of great interest, "Nelson and the Twentieth Century," by Arnold White and E. Hallam Moorhouse (Cassell. 5s. net), I take two passages typical of the authors' purposes, which are, first, to study Nelson and his great comrades, and, secondly, to apply his teaching to the present conditions of naval warfare.

The whole of the Trafalgar battle seems to centre round Nelson. Amid that setting of sea and sky, amid the thunder and flame of the guns, his last actions acquire an almost legendary glory. All that was petty, irritable, and unworthy dropped from his ardent spirit as he went into his last fight with steadfast composure and heroic resolution. He had a presentiment that he would fall. When in sight of the combined fleets of France and Spain he went to his cabin and wrote the prayer which summed up all his life, all his efforts, in the grave and noble words:

"May the Great God, whom I worship, grant to my country, and for the benefit of Europe in general, a great and glorious victory; and may no misconduct in anyone tarnish it; and may humanity after victory be the predominant feature in the British fleet.

For myself individually, I commit my life to Him who made me, and may His blessing light upon my endeavours for serving my country faithfully. To Him I resign myself, and the just cause which is entrusted to me to defend. Amen. Amen. Amen."

Lieutenant Pasco had come to the cabin to make a personal request as well as to present a report, but finding his Admiral on his knees, he waited in silence till Nelson rose, and then gave his report without troubling him about his private wishes, though they affected his chances of promotion—a restraint which shows the flag-lieutenant in a singularly attractive light.

It was this same Lieutenant Pasco who was associated with Nelson in the making of the immortal signal. In his own words: "I had the honour to suggest the substitution of the word 'expects' for 'confides.' Lord Nelson had chosen the latter, but it not being in the vocabulary, must have been spelt, and have taken more time than could have been spared (as we were close on the enemy), and the word 'expects' only required one number. After it had been answered, his Lordship ordered me to make the signal (No. 16) for close action, and to keep it flying."

42

## A Plea for More Nelson-Worship.

The second passage I have selected is as follows:

We celebrate the centenaries of nobodies, and write volumes on the achievements of the dilettante. In the metropolis visitors and Londoners gaze on a profusion of effigies of immortalised mediocrity. Of the fifty-nine principal statues in London some of the originals, when living, did nothing to maintain the Empire that Nelson's captains created. Only one spot in the capital is associated with the maritime history of England, but in Trafalgar Square there is nothing but the name to remind the passer-by of Nelson's magnificent "band of brothers." Its original purpose has been abandoned. For all that Trafalgar Square or London can show to the contrary, the Spanish Armada was never defeated: Lord Howard of Effingham, Raleigh, Hawkins, and Frobisher had no existence. How many Londoners know of Admiral Edward Russell, who fought the sixteen French men-of-war, and delivered England from the fear of foreign invasion; or of Hawke, who swooped down on the French at Quiberon? In Trafalgar Square Collingwood—Nelson's "dear Coll"—might justly have found a place. He brought the British fleet out of action at Trafalgar; but the capital of the Empire knows him not. If the Battle of Trafalgar had been won by France, the Admiral would have had an arch of triumph and each of his captains a street dedicated to his memory. Where British heroes of the sea ought to stand, statues of George IV. and Sir Charles Napier occupy places of honour. A sum of £30,000 would cover the cost of erecting statues to ten of our sea captains in Trafalgar Square, and of transferring the effigies of the three major-generals and the First Gentleman in Europe to fitter spots for the commemoration of their valour and their virtue.

In 1905 there are fresh reasons for dedicating Trafalgar Square to sea power and to Nelson. With the physique of the people deteriorated by the decay of agriculture and by the congestion of the great towns, only 23 per cent. of the population now dwell in the country. Therefore sea power is more important to an urban and an invalid population than in the days when British soldiers fought Bonaparte on British beef and beer, while British sailors drove Villeneuve from the sea. The masses are still suffered to remain ignorant of the history of their country and the secret of her power.

Germans taunt Great Britain with the fact that the average child is ignorant of the name of Nelson. One of them says: "At the time when your Navy League was reviving the memory of Trafalgar, I found that not one of these boys knew who Nelson was." He was referring to boys from Board Schools whom he had employed a few years before. The men whom we ought to honour and whom we have forgotten, themselves hoped for the recognition of posterity. At the battle of St. Vincent in 1797 Jervis exclaimed, "Look at Troubridge! He tacks his ship to battle as if the eyes of all England were on him—and would to God they were!" We may repeat, "And would to God they were!"

---

## The Most Picturesque Sea Fight in History.

The October magazines bear witness to the fast rising tide of enthusiasm for the Nelson Centenary. In the "Cornhill Magazine" the Rev. Mr. Fitchett, one of our most inspiring writers on Empire history, writes on "The Picturesque Side of Trafalgar." I quote a stirring passage:

Trafalgar is the most stately, impressive, and, in a sense, artistic sea-battle the world has seen, or ever will see. For sea-warfare to-day, if it has grown more terrible, has certainly grown more prosaic. It has lost its stateliness, its colour, its air of majesty. What can be less impressive for the artistic imagination than the modern ironclad; the low black or grey hull, the three squat funnels, the naked spars that serve for masts; the bare, unsheltered deck; the rounded, inexpressive stern? A column of modern ironclads resembles nothing so much as a procession of prize-fighters stripped for the ring: short-necked, bullet-headed, blunt-nosed, with mighty biceps and calves which suggest Caliban rather than Ariel or Apollo. There is strength in them; fighting efficiency, destructive power at its highest. It is probable that a single modern battle-ship of the second class could "take on" both the fleets that fought at Trafalgar, and —given sufficient sea-room—could sink both without having her paint spoiled; without even coming within reach of their guns. But what the modern fighting ship has gained in fighting power, it has lost in impressiveness and grace of aspect. Nothing could well be more majestic than the aspect of one of the great fleets that English admirals led to fight in the last years of the eighteenth century. The tall masts, the far-spread yards, the skyward-leaping piles of canvas, the leaning deck, the castle-like hull, the long, curving lines of guns rising above each other, the figured stern—here was all the glory of majestic form and varied colour! When two fleets of such ships were set in battle array by some great captain, the majesty of the scene was overwhelming. And this is the spectacle which Trafalgar offers. It is the old, picturesque, and majestic sea-fighting of the eighteenth century at its highest point. The sea has beheld no such spectacle since, nor ever will again.

## Nelson's Foresight.

It is remarkable, says W. Clark Russell in his "Life of Nelson," that long before Nelson sailed he should have thoroughly digested those very manœuvres which subsequently resulted in the overwhelming defeat of the combined fleets of France and Spain. He had, no doubt—true to his old custom—reviewed in his mind, during the many lonely hours he had spent in blockading and in chasing, every imaginable posture in which the enemy could offer himself; but it is astonishing to find human sagacity rising into absolute prophecy, as assuredly happened in the case of Nelson, who appears to have anticipated the exact order in which the confederated foe would appear. It is told in Dean Pellew's "Life of Lord Sidmouth" that shortly before Lord Nelson's departure, Lord Sidmouth wrote to ask him to take Richmond Park, on his way from Merton to London. Nelson sent this answer: "On Tuesday forenoon, if Superior Powers do not prevent me, I will be in Richmond Park, and shall be happy in taking you by the hand and to wish you a most perfect restoration to health." This was the last letter Lord Sidmouth ever received from his illustrious friend; he cherished it greatly, and wrote thus at the foot of it: " Lord

Nelson came on that day, and passed some hours at Richmond Park. This was our last meeting." In after years he used to relate to his friends the particulars of this interview. There was a little study-table in the room; Nelson went to it and scored diagrams upon it with his finger, to explain the manner in which, if the combined fleets offered to fight him, he proposed to attack them. "Rodney," he said, "broke the line in one point; I will break it in two." "There," Lord Sidmouth said, "there is the table on which he drew the plan of the battle of Trafalgar, but five weeks before his death. It is strange that I should have used this valued relic for above thirty years without having once thought of recording upon it a fact so interesting. Now I have perpetuated it by this brief record:

" 'On the 10th day of September, 1805, Vice-Admiral Lord Viscount Nelson described to Lord Sidmouth, upon this table, the manner in which he intended to engage the combined fleets of France and Spain, which he expected shortly to meet. He stated that he should attack them in two lines, led by himself and Admiral Collingwood, and felt confident that he should capture either their van and centre, on the 21st of October, following, in the glorious battle of Trafalgar.' "

❦ ❦ ❦

## The Knights of Trafalgar.
### To the Editor of T.P.'s WEEKLY.

Sir,—We hope that this year, 1905, the centenary of the Battle of Trafalgar, you will allow us, on behalf of the above-named institution, to appeal through your columns to all the benevolently disposed who would be glad to see the greatest naval event in our history associated with the beneficent work of relieving the distressed.

The society, on behalf of which we venture to address you, originated in 1809 in a lodge called "The Knights of Trafalgar," a title taken expressly to commemorate the great battle in which Nelson gave his life for his country. The Benevolent Society connected with the Lodge was amalgamated with the Spitalfields Benevolent Society in 1889. The object of the society is to provide funds for the distribution of bread and coals—absolutely without distinction of religious denominations—among the poor of London during the winter months of each year, and it is supported by donations, as well as by the subscription of members.

Whilst it distributed in 1904 the sum of £588 in the purchase of bread and coals, its regular expenses amounted to £38 only, owing to there being no paid officers. Donations, therefore, reached the beneficiaries almost undiminished. Many distinguished names will be found on the list of the society's patrons and benefactors.

Those who are willing to subscribe to its funds are requested to send their donations to the London and County Bank, Shoreditch Branch, E.C.—Your obedient servants,

WALTER T. KEW,
C. H. SEYMOUR,
Admirals of the Fleet.
CYPRIAN A. G. BRIDGE, Admiral.

## October 20, 1905.

NELSONIANA

1805    1905

"THANK GOD, I HAVE DONE MY DUTY."

### The Death of Nelson.

O'er Nelson's tomb, with silent grief
   oppress'd,
Britannia mourns her hero now at rest ;
But those bright laurels ne'er shall fade
   with years,
Whose leaves, whose leaves are water'd
   by a nation's tears.

'Twas in Trafalgar's Bay,
We saw the foemen lay,
   Each heart was bounding then ;
We scorn'd the foreign yoke,
For our ships were British oak,
   And hearts of oak our men.
Our Nelson mark'd them on the wave,
Three cheers our gallant seamen gave,
   Nor thought of home or beauty.
Along the line the signal ran—
" England expects, that ev'ry man
This day will do his duty."

And now the cannons roar
Along the affright'd shore ;
   Our Nelson led the way ;
His ship the *Vict'ry* named,
Long be that *Vict'ry* famed,
   For vict'ry crown'd the day.
But dearly was the conquest bought,
Too well the gallant hero fought,
   For England, home, and beauty,
He cried, as 'midst the fire he ran—
" England expects, that ev'ry man
This day will do his duty."

At last the fatal wound,
Which spread dismay around,
   The hero's breast received.
" Heav'n fights on our side !
The day's our own," he cried !
   " Now long enough I've lived !
In honour's cause my life was pass'd,
In honour's cause I fall at last,
   For England, home, and beauty."
Thus ending life as he began,
England confessed, that ev'ry man
   That day had done his duty.

S. J. ARNOLD.

## The Death of Nelson.

The following was Dr. Beatty's deeply touching account of Nelson's death:

The captain ordered the seamen to carry the admiral to the cockpit; and now two incidents occurred strikingly characteristic of the great man, and strongly marking that energy and reflection which in his heroic mind rose even superior to the immediate consideration of his awful condition. While the men were carrying him down the ladder from the middle-deck his lordship observed that the tiller-ropes were not yet replaced, and desired one of the midshipmen stationed there to go up on the quarter-deck and remind Captain Hardy of that circumstance, and request that new ones should be immediately rove. Having delivered this order, he took his handkerchief from his pocket and covered his face with it, that he might be conveyed to the cockpit at this crisis unnoticed by the crew. . . . The surgeon had examined these two officers, and found them dead, when his attention was arrested by several of the wounded calling to him, "Mr. Beatty, Lord Nelson is here; Mr. Beatty, the admiral is wounded." The surgeon, on looking round, saw the handkerchief fall from his lordship's face, when the stars on his coat, which had also been covered by it, appeared. Mr. Burke, the purser, and the surgeon ran immediately to his lordship's assistance, and took him from the arms of the seamen who had carried him below. In conveying him to one of the midshipmen's berths they stumbled, but recovered themselves without falling. Lord Nelson then inquired who were supporting him, and when the surgeon informed him his lordship replied, "Ah, Mr. Beatty! you can do nothing for me. I have but a short time to live; my back is shot through." The surgeon said "He hoped the wound was not so dangerous as his lordship imagined, and that he might still survive long enough to enjoy his glorious victory." The Rev. Dr. Scott, who had been in another part of the cockpit administering lemonade to the wounded, now came instantly to his lordship, and in his anguish of grief wrung his hands and said, "Ah, Beatty! how prophetic you were!" alluding to the apprehensions expressed by the surgeon for his lordship's safety previous to the battle.

## "It is all over."

His lordship was laid upon a bed, stripped of his clothes, and covered with a sheet. While this was effecting he said to Dr. Scott, "Doctor, I told you so; I am gone," and after a short pause he added, in a low voice, "I have to leave Lady Hamilton and my adopted daughter Horatia as a legacy to my country." (Dr. Beatty then describes the examination of the wound, and that, from Lord Nelson's symptoms as described by himself, the case was hopeless, but that this was not told to Lord Nelson until the victory had been certain, and communicated to him.)

Then came an ardent thirst. He called frequently for drink and to be fanned with paper: "Fan, fan, drink, drink." This he continued to do until a very few minutes before he expired. Mr. Burke told him the enemy were decisively defeated, and that he hoped he would still live to be the bearer of the joyful news. "It is nonsense, Mr. Burke, to suppose I can live. My sufferings are great, but they will all be soon over." Dr. Scott entreated him not "to despair of living," and said "he trusted that Divine Providence would restore him once more to his dear country and friends." "Ah, doctor!" he replied, "it is all over—it is all over."

## "How goes the day?"

Many messages were sent to Captain Hardy by the surgeon, requesting his attendance on his lordship, who had become impatient, and often exclaimed, "Will no one bring Hardy to me? He must be killed; he is surely destroyed." The captain's aide-de-camp now came below (Mr. Bulkeley), and stated that circumstances respecting the fleet required Hardy's presence on deck, but that he would avail himself of the first favourable moment to come. On hearing him say this to the surgeon, Nelson asked who had brought it. "It is Mr. Bulkeley, my lord," said Mr. Burke. "It is his voice," said Nelson; and then to Bulkeley, "Remember me to your father." After about an hour and ten minutes Hardy came.

They shook hands affectionately, and then Nelson said, "Well, Hardy, how goes the battle? How goes the day with us?" "Very well, my lord; we have got twelve or fourteen of the

46

enemy's ships in our possession; but five of their van have tacked, and show an intention of bearing down on the Victory. I have, therefore, called two or three of our fresh ships round us, and have no doubt of giving them a good drubbing." "I hope," said Nelson, "none of our ships have struck, Hardy!" "No, my lord; there is no fear of that." Nelson then said, "Hardy, I am a dead man. Hardy, I am going fast; it will be all over with me soon. Come near to me. Pray let dear Lady Hamilton have my hair, and all other things belonging to me." Mr. Burke was about to withdraw at the beginning of this conversation, but Nelson, perceiving his intention, desired him to remain. Captain Hardy observed "that he hoped Mr. Beatty could yet hold out some prospect of life." "Oh, no; it is impossible. My back is shot through. Beatty will tell you so." After a parting shake of the hand, Hardy returned to the deck.

## "I have done my duty."

About fifty minutes after, Hardy returned. They again shook hands, and while the captain retained Nelson's hand he congratulated him, even in the arms of death, on his brilliant victory, which, he said, was complete, though he did not know how many of the enemy were captured, as it was impossible to perceive each ship distinctly. He was certain, however, of fourteen or fifteen having surrendered. "That is well, but I bargained for twenty," and then, emphatically, "Anchor, Hardy! Anchor!" To this Hardy replied, "I suppose, my lord, Admiral Collingwood will now take upon himself the direction of affairs?" "Not while I live, I hope, Hardy," cried the dying chief, and at that moment tried ineffectually to raise himself from his bed. "No," added he; "do you anchor, Hardy." "Shall we make the signal, sir?" "Yes; for if I live I'll anchor." He then told Captain Hardy "he felt in a few minutes he should be no more," adding, in low tone, "Don't throw me overboard." "Oh, no, certainly not," replied Hardy. "Then you know what to do," and he continued, "Take care of my dear Lady Hamilton; take care of poor Lady Hamilton. Kiss me, Hardy." The captain now knelt down, and kissed his cheek, when Nelson said, "Now I am satisfied. Thank God, I have done my duty." Hardy stood for a moment or two in silent contemplation. He knelt down again, and kissed his lordship's forehead. Nelson said, "Who is that?" "It is Hardy," answered the captain. "God bless you, Hardy!" After this affecting scene Hardy withdrew, and returned to the quarter-deck.

## "God and my country."

The narrative is thus concluded by Nelson's chaplain, Dr. Scott:

After this, the Admiral was perfectly tranquil—looking at me in his accustomed manner when alluding to any prior discourse. "I have not been a great sinner, doctor," said he. "Doctor, I was right—I told you so—George Rose has not yet got my letter. Tell him "—he was here interrupted by pain. After an interval he said, "Mr. Rose will remember. Don't forget, doctor. Mind what I say." There were frequent pauses in his conversation. These sentences refer to what he had told Dr. Scott in his first interview. When I first saw him he was apprehensive he should not live many minutes, and told me so, adding, in a hurried, agitated manner, though with pauses, "Remember me to Lady Hamilton—remember me to Horatia—remember me to all my friends. Doctor, remember me to Mr. Rose: tell him I have made a will and left Lady Hamilton and Horatia to my country." He repeated his remembrances to Lady Hamilton and Horatia, and told me to mind what he said several times.

The confusion of the scene, the pain endured by the hero, and the necessity of alleviating his sufferings by giving lemonade to quench his thirst, and by rubbing his body, of course precluded the reading of prayers to him in a regular form, but otherwise during the three hours and a half of Nelson's mortal agony they ejaculated short prayers together, and Nelson frequently said, "Pray for me, doctor." Every interval, indeed, allowed by the intense pain, and not taken up in the conduct of the action or in the mention of his own private affairs, was thus employed in low and earnest supplication for Divine mercy. The last words which Dr. Scott heard murmured on his lips were, "God and my country," and he passed so quietly out of life that Scott, who had been occupied ever since he had been brought below in all the offices of the most tender nurse, was still rubbing his stomach when the surgeon perceived that all was over.

## Died of his Wound.

These are the simple words in the Victory's log-book recording Nelson's death : " Partial firing continued until 4.30, when a victory having been reported to the Right Honourable Lord Viscount Nelson, K.B., he died of his wound."

## Only one Nelson.

Other men have died in the hour of victory, but for no other has victory so singular and so signal graced the fulfilment and ending of a great life's work. "Finis coronat opus" has of no man been more true than of Nelson. There were, indeed, consequences momentous and stupendous yet to flow from the decisive supremacy of Great Britain's sea-power, the establishment of which, beyond all question or competition, was Nelson's great achievement; but his part was done when Trafalgar was fought. The coincidence of his death with the moment of completed success has impressed upon that superb battle a stamp of finality, an immortality of fame, which even its own grandeur scarcely could have insured. He needed, and he left, no successor. To use again St. Vincent's words, "There is but one Nelson."—Captain Mahan.

## His Home.

It seems strange and melancholy that at the very time when the heart of the nation is with its old hero, Nelson's house at Merton is on the market and has an uncertain fate to meet. The Rev. Francis M. Anderson has recently written a plea for the acquisition of this fine old house by the nation. He says:

The house will probably be demolished and the land built over. This house was Nelson's home, the home he loved and prized. Surely some steps ought to be taken to secure the property for the nation. At Merton, Nelson entertained his Nile captains and other friends; the place is very full of precious memories. Many others, like myself, have doubtless paced the long, broad gravel walk, stretching the whole length of the garden, called by Nelson his "quarterdeck." Inside the house the association deepens; against these very mantelpieces he has often leaned; the fires that burned below them have often welcomed him and his friends; the staircase is the one up which he flew to take a last fond look at his little daughter and to pray over the sleeping child in her cot : the door which closed upon him as the chaise bore him off on his last journey to Portsmouth, shut him out for ever from his "dear, dear Merton." In the neighbourhood to-day it is erroneously supposed that the house belonged to Lady Hamilton, and that Nelson himself did not actually reside there. This is not the case; the house was Nelson's very own.

## Burial.

The "Victory," with the remains of the ever-to-be-lamented Nelson, arrived off Sheerness, Sunday, December 22, 1805. The body was placed the following morning on board the "Chatham" yacht, proceeding on her way to Greenwich. The coffin, covered with an ensign, was placed on deck. Tuesday she arrived at Greenwich; the body, still being in the coffin made of the wreck of "L'Orient," was then enveloped in the colours of the "Victory," bound round by a piece of rope, and carried by sailors, part of the crew of the "Victory," to the Painted Hall, where preparations were made for the lying in state; the days appointed for which were Sunday, Monday, and Tuesday, January 5, 6, and 7, 1806, and to which all due effect was given. Wednesday, January 8, the first day's procession by water took place, and the remains were removed from Greenwich to Whitehall, and from thence to the Admiralty, with all possible pomp and solemnity. This procession of barges, &c., was nearly a mile long, minute guns being fired during its progress. The banner of emblems was borne by Captain Hardy, Lord Nelson's captain. The body was deposited that night in the captain's room at the Admiralty, and attended by the Rev. John Scott.

Thursday, January 9, 1806, the procession from the Admiralty to St. Paul's moved forward about eleven o'clock in the morning, the first part consisting of cavalry regiments, regimental bands with muffled drums, Greenwich pensioners, seamen from the "Victory," about 200 mourning coaches, 400 carriages of public officers, nobility, &c., including those of the royal family (the Prince of Wales, Duke of Clarence, &c., taking part in the procession). The body, upon a funeral car, was drawn by six led horses. At Temple Bar, the city officers took their places in the procession. Upon arrival at the cathedral, they entered by the west gate and the great west door, ranging themselves according to their ranks. The seats were as follows: under the dome, in each archway, in the front of the piers, and in the gallery over the choir. The form of the seats under the dome took the shape of the dome, namely, a circular appearance, and calculated to hold 3,056 persons; an iron railing was also placed from the dome to the great western door, within which persons were allowed to stand. The body was placed on a bier, erected on a raised platform opposite to the eagle desk. At the conclusion of the service in the choir, a procession was formed from thence to the grave, with banners, &c. The interment being over, Garter proclaimed the style; and the comptroller, treasurer, and steward of the deceased, breaking their staves, gave the pieces to Garter, who threw them into the grave.

The procession, arranged by the officers of arms, then returned.

For a few days after the public were admitted upon a shilling fee, and permitted to enter the enclosed spot directly over the body, looking down a distance of about ten feet, and were gratified with a sight of the coffin, placed upon a sort of table covered with black cloth.—"Notes and Queries," October 9, 1852.

## What Nelson Said.

Only recollect that a brave man dies but once, but a coward all his life long.

Whatever plans may be adopted, the moment the enemy touch our coast, be it where it may, they are to be attacked by every man afloat and on shore; this must be perfectly understood. Never fear the event.

Nothing can stop the courage of English seamen.

In sea affairs, nothing is impossible, and nothing improbable.

London has so many charms, that a man's time is wholly taken up.

A Norfolk man is as good as two others.

Women always will do as they please. Orders are not for them—at least, I never yet knew one who obeyed.

I am of opinion that the boldest measures are the safest.

To fret yourself to death, because you believe that all the world are not so honest as yourself, is useless, for you cannot reform it, were you an angel, and it makes people sorry to see you torment yourself.

Not being a man of fortune is a crime which I cannot get over; and, therefore, none of the Great care about me. . . . Notwithstanding the neglect I have met with, I am happy, and now I see the propriety of not having built my hopes on such sandy foundations as the friendships of the Great.

A little farm and my good name form all my wants and wishes .

Thank God. I have done my duty.

## The Last Three from Trafalgar.

This superb sonnet was written by Dante Gabriel Rossetti for an anniversary banquet given in memory of Trafalgar some thirty years ago. Three veteran naval officers, who had been present at the battle, were among the company:

In grappled ships around the Victory
  Three boys did England's duty with
    stout cheer,
  While one dread truth was kept from
    every ear,
More dire than deafening fire that
  churned the sea;
For in the flagship's weltering cockpit,
  he
Who was the battle's heart without a
  peer,
He who had seen all fearful sights
  save Fear,
Was passing from all life save Victory.

And round the old memorial board
  to-day
  Three greybeards—each a warworn
    British tar—
  View through the mist of years that
    hour afar;
Who soon shall greet, 'mid memories of
  fierce fray,
The impassioned soul which on its
  radiant way
  Soared through the fiery cloud of
    Trafalgar.

# LAST LINKS WITH NELSON.

*To the Editor of* T.P.'s WEEKLY.

Sir,—To the many interesting stories and entertaining matter in connection with England's greatest sailor, which have from time to time appeared in your paper, may I be allowed to contribute one or two facts? My maternal grandmother, Mrs. John Walls, née Silvester, spent some years of her childhood at the dawn of the nineteenth century in the pleasant and then rural village of Merton, Surrey. She had a very distinct recollection of the place and its surroundings. She told me that for some time she was at a small preparatory school there with the young "Horatia," whose name and whose future were uppermost in the thoughts of the dying Nelson on that sad yet glorious day, October 21, 1805. There was not, she said, a doubt in the minds of the villagers that the child so frequently and tenderly alluded to in his letters by the distinguished admiral as "my dear Horatia" was his natural daughter, and not an adopted one. She described the young lady as being very pleasant in manner, and favoured with good looks. In passing, I here wish to correct statements that have occasionally appeared in your paper and others that the residence known as "Abbey" or "Merton Abbey" House was the home of Nelson, from which he departed never to return on the memorable 13th September, 1805. Sir William Hamilton for a time rented "Merton Abbey" House, and the naval hero stayed there frequently with him and the beautiful, fascinating "Emma."

### A man who remembered Nelson.

The particular house, with its grounds, on which the admiral lavished a great deal of money, was known as "Merton Place," and was demolished many years ago. In 1873 I went to Merton, for the first time, actuated by a desire to see a place where my relative's youth was spent, and the "dear, dear Merton" of the immortal Nelson, where, to quote a passage in his "Diary," "I left all that I hold dear in this world to go and serve my king and country." On the occasion of my visit, I interviewed an elderly lady, a resident of the parish, and who was well posted up in its traditions. She kindly pointed out to me a portion of the site where "Merton Place" once stood. A few mean-looking houses were built on the spot, and the small garden plots in the rear formed part, she said, of the original grounds of Lord Nelson's abode. At that time there was living at Merton a very old man, a native of the village, who remembered the Hamiltons and the great admiral well. Unfortunately I did not meet with him, but the lady I saw knew him intimately. I should not have dilated on this subject, but a correspondent in your issue of the 20th ult. writes as if "Merton Abbey" House, occupied for a time by the late popular "Gaiety" favourite, Miss Kate Vaughan, was Nelson's last home in England, and one that should be purchased by the nation as a memorial for all time of him who did so much for Britain and the world at large. To make a place which he only rented a "Mecca" for his admirers to journey to would, I venture to think, be foolish. There are many historic houses in England where he stayed. As another link with the great naval past, my grandfather, John Walls, happened to be at Portsmouth in 1805, and was one of the first to go on board the Victory when she arrived on December 4 in that memorable year with the remains of Nelson. He graphically described to me, a most interested listener, the battered condition of the historic vessel, which showed traces of the dreadful slaughter enacted in Trafalgar's Bay. I have in my possession a few miniature toys carved by a French prisoner-of-war, who was captured in the great fight, and subsequently kept "in durance vile" with many others of his country in Porchester Castle, Hants.

### The dying request.

These interesting trifles were purchased there in 1806. A relative of my aforesaid grandfather, one Richard Walls, was a warrant-officer under Nelson, and was drowned in the Straits of Gibraltar at the end of the eighteenth century, whilst serving in the fleet. To me there is another interesting circumstance, which was told to me by the before-mentioned Mrs. John Walls. Her father was one of the few spectators who saw, off Spithead, the Royal George go down on August 29, 1782. I have read a great many reminiscences in connection with Lord Nelson and Lady Hamilton, but I humbly think that there is no one living, with the exception of myself, who has spoken with a lady who was at school with the child whom Nelson, in his last moments, desired should be an object of solicitude and care to his country. Alas! the nation, and those who benefited financially by the hero's death and glorious services, ignored his dying and pathetic wishes. History repeated itself. Did not the " Merry Monarch," when his end was drawing near, say, " Let not poor Nellie starve," or words to that effect, alluding to Mistress Nell Gwynne? Thousands wended their way to the historic square on the 21st inst., but how i may of those pilgrims knew that the col :mn was not a fact accomplished till 1843! Again a lapse of time— twenty-four years—before Landseer's lions were added, and the memorial completed, viz., in 1867. Shakespeare truly says: " The good is oft interred with their bones."

THOMAS CHARLES WALLS.

---

## Nelson and Family History.

*To the Editor of* T.P.'s WEEKLY.

Sir,—So long as hero-worship lingers as a special feature of Englishmen, and the pride of patriotism finds expression in commemorating the death of our heroes, so long will interest be taken in any details concerning Nelson ; I should, therefore, like to say—as one who claims a direct connection with the sea-power of the past—that my grandfather, Admiral Thomas Gill, was a young officer, and afterwards captain, who took part in the great battles of Nelson's era. For many years when ashore he lived at Bath, where he was a notable figure : he lived to be ninety-three, and died in 1874, " The Father of the Navy." Gill was a fighting captain of the true Nelsonian type, and a man of resource. As lieutenant he was appointed to the Victory, but by an accident was left behind with Lieutenant Symonds, who followed in another man-of-war. In the paper

" Chic," of February 4, 1905, was a portrait of Admiral Gill, and also one of his daughter, Miss Gill—still living at Portsmouth—where it will be seen that, like Nelson, Gill was a one-armed man, for he had lost his left arm in the capture of La Lodi as sub-lieutenant of the Racoon. In 1830 Gill was a Post Captain of H.M.S. Magnificent, after serving on twenty-five men-of-war and commanding eight. He knew Lord Nelson personally, for each lived opposite the other in St. George's Square, Portsmouth, which town, as Admiral Sir Cyprian Bridge remarked on " Trafalgar Day," had unique connection with Lord Nelson ; indeed, when ashore the great hero stayed at " Nelson House," known by two hens on the roof. Moreover, Gill and Nelson often dined together.

### *His knife and fork.*

Miss Gill, into whose possession " Nelson House " came, writing in May, 1905, says :

My father was dining with him, and Nelson remarked the discomfort of putting his knife down each time. " Look at mine, knife and fork in one; will you please accept it? I'm going to town to-morrow, and will get another. They are made for me." Father accepted, and used it ever after to his death. This, the original combined knife and fork, is in the possession of the family, as alike Nelson's signature; but the second Nelson knife and fork alluded to above is to be seen at Earl's Court Exhibition.

Now, Admiral Gill's wife was a Miss Symonds, grand-daughter of Sir Geo. Rooke, Bart., who took Gibraltar from the Spaniards. Lord Nelson, like Gill, might have attained, had he been spared, the ease and dignity of an early retirement. Yet he fell not prematurely whose work was done at the heat of noon, at the full tide of human success, and at the height of manhood's fame. For, as Southey says : " The most triumphant death is that of the martyr, the most splendid that of the hero in the hour of victory ! " For truly :

He left a name at which the world grew pale,
To point a moral or adorn a tale!

HERBERT H. SMITH, M.D.

# INDEX

**Nelson, Adm Horatio, Lord**

death, 2, 39, 46-7, 48; sense of fame, 2; coffin, 3; nightcap, 3; in Quebec, 3; 'England expects..', 4, 34, 40, 42; with children, 4; off Cadiz, 4; health, 5; German Generals, 5; hat, 5; meets Wellington, 5; in Coventry, 6; eulogy from Liverpool, 7; with Emma, 9; stealing pears, 10; first name, 10; body at Greenwich, 11, 14; his spy, 12; walrus episode, 12; sayings, 13, 23; relative of Wellington's, 13; fondness of fishing, 13; poetry, 14, 20; at cowes, 18; uniform at Trafalgar, 18; funeral, 19, 30; an apple seller, 20; his upholsterer, 23; in Birmingham, 23; his will, 24; at Boulogne, 25; promotion of a Midshipman, 27; brick at school, 27; portraiture, 28; off Toulon, 29, 31; prayer before Trafalgar, 34, 42; dance in VICTORY, 36; forewarned of death, 41; meets Lord Sidmouth, 44

Nelson, Susannah, 15
Nelson, William, 1st Earl, 2, 4
Nelson's column, London, 10
Nicolas, Sir Nicholas Harris, 3, 8, 19, 31
Nile, battle of, 3, 9, 13, 22, 23, 28, 33, 37
NORTHUMBERLAND (74), 28
Parker, Adm Sir Hyde, 22, 26
Parsons, Lt Ramsey, 12, 28
Pasco, Lt John, 40, 42
Paston Grammar School, 27
Peard, Capt Shuldham, 29
Pettigrew, Dr Thomas J, 9
PHOEBE (frigate), 29
RACEHORSE (frigate), 12
Railton, William, 10
RAISONNABLE (64), 2
REDOUBTABLE (Fr 74), 39
Rider, Jack, 9
Rodney, Adm Lord, 38
Romney, Sir George, 19

Rose, George, 47
Rowlandson, Thomas, 41
Rowsell, Midshipman, 40
ROYAL SOVEREIGN (100), 40
Russell, W Clark, 7, 26, 44
ST GEORGE (98), 26
St Paul's Cathedral, 36
St Vincent, battle of, 7, 8, 22, 43
St Vincent, Earl, 7, 8, 9, 24, 48
SAN JOSEF (Sp 112), 8, 22
SAN NICOLAS (Sp 80), 8, 22
SANTISSIMA TRINIDAD (Sp 130), 8, 22, 39
Scott, Dr Alexander, 9
Scott, Rev John, 46, 47
Sixtyninth Regiment, 8
Sladen, Douglas, 41, 42
Southey, Sir Robert, 3, 10, 12, 14, 23, 32
Stephen, Deemster, 41
SUCCESS (frigate), 29
Suckling, Capt Maurice, 2, 16
SWIFTSURE (74), 3, 31
Ticknor, George, 2
Trafalgar, battle of, 34, 37, 38, 39, 40, 41, 42, 43, 44; blockade of Cadiz, 7; Knights of, 44
Trafalgar Bay, 12
Trafalgar Day, 2, 51
Treville, Latouche (Fr Adm), 29
Troubridge, Sir Thomas, 8, 43
VANGUARD (74), 3
VICTORY (100), 8, 9, 24, 27, 30, 31, 36, 38-9, 40, 41, 47, 48
Villeneuve, Pierre (Fr Adm), 26, 37, 43
Wallace, Duncan, 22, 25
Walls, Richard, 50
Walpole family, 16
Ward, Horatia (nee Thompson and Nelson), 24, 46, 47
Wellington, Duke of, 5, 7, 13, 36, 37
Welmos (sic, Dane), 6
West, Benjamin, 2
White, Arnold and Moorhouse, E Hallam, 33, 42
ZEALAND (Danish 74), 40